MARKETING MATTERS

Daniel Rendelman

DEDICATION

To my friends at Best Version Media, from whom many of these ideas originated. You are truly passionate about bringing people together all throughout North America as you make a difference in local communities. The tenacity and grit you each exhibit are inspiring. There's really nothing new in the pages of this book – only borrowed concepts we have learned together which are hopefully presented in a new way.

To my wife Sara, who encourages my learning and inspires me to be the best version of myself. You never once complained of the many hours that were poured into this book. Instead, you urged me to write and often made time for me to focus. I couldn't ask for a more supportive and loving partner – for business and life.

TABLE OF CONTENTS

THE BIGGEST PROBLEM SOLVED

Believe it or not, your company's number one problem is not employee issues, lack of product, customer retention, economic swings, or cash flow. It is not even rumors of wars or lockdowns from a medical condition. No, the biggest challenge any company faces is... obscurity.

The most significant dilemma for your business is nothing new – it's the same issue you confronted when you first started. Not enough people or not the right people know about your brand. Best-selling author and entrepreneur, Grant Cardone agrees, "Obscurity is the single biggest killer of a business, and it's a bigger problem than money." Obscurity causes companies to go under and great ideas never to be acted upon by potential or existing customers.

How do you overcome this war against obscurity? First, you must realize most people don't know about your company! Because you work the business daily, it is easy to think everyone in town knows your location or services. This colossal mistake stops you from reaching out and grabbing attention. To beat obscurity, you must brand long-term. This is why we all recognize national brands like State Farm, BMW and Amazon, who keep their logo and tagline before us.

Recently, the Institute of Practitioners in Advertising (IPA) found that in the 2008 recession, brands that "went dark" (stopped advertising and communicating with consumers for one year) suffered considerable financial consequences for six months or more and took five years to recover and return to their expected profits. Companies that cut their ad budgets in half for one year took three years to recover. Research has proven that marketing doesn't cost – it pays. And it pays long-term.

Obscurity is overcome by recognition. Marketing works to increase your recognition compellingly so that the community knows who you are and feels good about your brand. The only effective way to increase your "market share" is to improve your "mind share" through marketing. Do you have a plan for engaging the community? If not, then you and your company are slowly becoming increasingly obscure. When your name is not in front of your ideal audience, it opens the door for your competition to compete. Insignificance will creep in without intentional promotion. Don't ignore the threat to your company's stability and growth - face obscurity with an action plan for marketing. Confront your real business problem with confidence!

PLAN YOUR WORK &
WORK YOUR PLAN

It didn't take long for the videos to go viral. Clips of iphones, golf balls, rake handles and other items that you wouldn't typically associate with being placed in blender were shared millions of times. This "Will it Blend?" campaign led to increased brand awareness and a boost in sales of the Blendtec kitchen utensil.

The creative and engaging videos generated significant attention and showed the strength and capabilities of their high-performance blenders. A simple product became a marketing success through an exact plan.

Everyone wants to grow their business, but many companies do not have an exact plan - they hope customers will find them. Hope is great, but it is not a business strategy!

An effective growth plan must include advertising. Companies like Apple, Geico, and Coca-Cola have expanded their branding approach for years. Your business can do the same. Branding is remembering. Your plan to help people remember to use your services or buy your products can be simple. Here are four easy ways to get started on your personal program:

Define your brand. Do you know you? Do your customers know you? By defining the exact purpose of your company first, you can decide on the visual elements that best reflect your mission. Answer these questions:

- Why are you in business?

- How do you bring value or benefit to your clients?

- What exactly do you do?

- What describes or defines you?

- Which colors, symbols, logos, or ideals represent you?

- What is your mission statement?

A study published in the *Harvard Business Review* found that businesses with strong brands outperformed their peers regarding revenue growth and profitability.

Determine your target market. Who are your perfect clients? Reaching homeowners is different than reaching tourists or children. Identify your exact clientele and pursue them in a way that emotionally connects with them. Be precise with your determination. How narrowly can you define your perfect customer? Brainstorm and then describe who buys now and who you want to buy. Determine and be specific with a statement like: "Female local residents with an average household income of over $80,000 and at least two children are my perfect client."

Decide on a platform to reach those exact people. Find a vehicle that positively carries and reinforces your message. The platform to reach moms with two children differs significantly from the platform that successfully markets to teenagers who listen to death-metal music. Effective marketing is more about creating loyal fans than attracting new clients with discounted offers. Your platform isn't singular. Don't put all your ads in one place! Print and digital ads work great together. Consider promotional giveaway items, sponsorship of local events, directional signage, social media posts, and display advertising.

Deliver your brand with a simple message and deliver it with repetition. Long-term exposure creates long-term results. The more touches your brand or logo has upon your target market, the more those customers are apt to think of you when they need you. Use the KISS method – "Keep it Stupid Simple." A catchy slogan or headline describing how you benefit the public is much better than a list of services you offer. The less you include in your advertisement, the more is remembered. It would not work for Baskin Robbins to advertise a list of 31 individual ice cream flavors. It does work for Baskin Robbins to say, "31 flavors."

You'll discover a complete marketing guide at the end of this book. Use this tool to enhance your company recognition and grow your bottom line.

ARE YOU PICKING UP PENNIES OR DOLLARS?

Here is a scenario.

You are driving along a highway, behold, you come across thousands of pennies lying on the road and an open suitcase with hundred-dollar bills blowing away.

Do you...

A) Run and start picking up pennies?

B) Run for the hundred-dollar bills?

98% of small business owners proverbially run and pick up pennies and let the $100 bills blow away! How?

Time is a limited resource but when used, it cannot be repurchased at any price. Take a plumber, for example. No one can be in 2 places at once. A plumber makes about $150 an hour. Yet, many will steal 5 hours of potentially billable time ($750 worth) to do 5 hours of bookkeeping or payroll (outsourced would cost $25 per hour - $125), costing them $625 in lost opportunity cost. That plumber just picked up pennies and let dollars blow away!

Another far too common task business owners do is DIY, or Do It Yourself, marketing.

Marketing pays nothing per hour to the business owner. That's a huge lost opportunity. Worse yet, most people need more experience in profitable, effective marketing. They haven't managed marketing before. That plumber knows how to

[6]

fix leaky pipes or running toilets. The plumber doesn't necessarily know how to reach his target market.

 By not focusing on core business and doing what makes money, that company is picking up pennies and letting $100 bills blow away in the wind. Don't let this happen to you. Define your target market and decide on the most effective ways to reach those people. Then deliver your message consistently. Perhaps partner with a media company who specializes in local businesses so you can focus on your own business. You will be more successful and have the dollars to prove it.

Cheaper Isn't Better

No one would choose a surgeon just because the doctor is cheaper than others. That idea is absurd. Sadly though, business owners often choose cheap advertising options with hopes of a miracle return. Cheaper isn't better in life or marketing.

Imagine you're a jewelry store, and you spend $300 on advertising with a coupon or special offer to the masses. You may get a response, and you may not. With that coupon offer, both the marketing expense and the discounted coupon response cost you profit. You've effectively spent money to lose money. Now imagine you're in the same jewelry store, and you spend $600 on advertising to a hot targeted market of jewelry buyers with a branded message that sets you apart. You attract high-end buyers with disposable income to pay top dollar. Instead of a gimmicky sales coupon or QR code, you advertise *about* the client and reach them in a memorable way. Which do you think is more effective long term?

The old saying is true – "you get what you pay for." Premium advertising is an investment that ensures your logo is seen. There are inexpensive ways to go from the mailbox to the trash can, but who wants to waste money? We all sort mail into two piles – one of junk and the other is full of items of importance. Traditional direct mail or coupon clippers have a national average response rate of less than 1.75%. A magazine with a large circulation doesn't help if the open rate is low. The same is true with television or radio at nonpeak hours. The price is higher for primetime or drivetime than middle-of-the-night airtime. Why? Because these are more valuable and more effective times to reach clients. Cheap advertising often means money is spent, but your ad is never seen.

If you're intentional, you can reach your ideal audience effectively without breaking the bank. One of the most valuable ways to get more from your exposure is to pair it with engaging content. This allows your marketing to magnetically pull people in with interest. It is the opposite of pushing out a noisy message that is immediately ignored. That pesky pop-up is easily swiped off the screen, while a feel-good story next to your ad draws people to your brand. To have your logo or image accompany engaging content is genius. Impressions stick when your ad is seen next to a compelling narrative, school, or non-profit because of the emotional connection established. Of course, there is a cost to provide this content. Ad space is usually at a higher premium when it's presented exceptionally because it is more beneficial as there are limited opportunities for space.

Just consider how you chose a service for yourself – are you looking for the absolute lowest cost or the best quality? Is your company the cheapest price in your industry, or do you consider yourself the most excellent? The chances are high that your clients will make buying decisions in a similar way. It is indeed odd that many business owners choose inexpensive methods to reach people and then are frustrated with the results. Just because something is less costly doesn't mean it is more effective.

THE LESS SAID, BEST SAID

English novelist Jane Austen, who penned classics like *Sense and Sensibility* and *Pride and Prejudice*, once wrote, "The less said, the better." And while that comment might seem odd from a verbose author, it makes perfect sense regarding advertising. If you want your ad to have an impact, you should make it simple and concise. It may seem counterintuitive but say less to be remembered more.

In today's world of an eight-second attention span, clarity is king. Too many words can drown out your message and turn off consumers. A simple logo, catchphrase, single-sentence testimonial, or exciting image is effective. That's all you need! Haven't you zoned out while commercials aired side effects or disclaimers? The same happens when you try to cram too much in a print or digital ad. Simple says it all. No one can read a wordy billboard. Busy flyers or websites are just as bad. Here's some advice - cut out calls to action asking people to "mention this ad" or "buy today." Show why your company is special instead of talking about your specials. And don't waste space on information that buyers can find when they Google you like an email address or even physical address.

You should keep a consistent brand image with easy-to-remember concepts and colors to get the most from your marketing dollars. Exciting language – like "just do it" – which is found in a short phrase can be easily remembered. A list of your services is often forgotten. We all know the slogans of national insurance companies that use a lizard to tell us they can save a certain percentage or blue colors and a deep voiceover saying that we are in "good hands." These basic ideas are chosen, repeated, and made clear. Those same insurance companies could list dozens of services or quote exact prices in their ads, but they don't. Neither should you. Personalize your spot to grab more exposure, and repeat, repeat, repeat.

Trust is built over time, so the more you are in front of your target audience, the more trust and reliability you can create.

When you are advertising, you aren't writing a novel; instead, you are trying to grab attention to grow awareness. Now more than ever, it's important to consider attention spans with marketing. Less is always more. Jane Austen was right.

THE ONE AND ONLY WAY TO TRACK ADVERTISING

Did you hear about the guy who was making counterfeit money and accidentally printed a bunch of $21 bills? He decided to go to a small-town gas station where the cashier wasn't too bright and see about exchanging them for real cash. He got there and asked the cashier for his change, and the cashier responded, "Not a problem. Do you want 7 - $3 bills or 3 - $7 bills?"

Fake bills might not be a problem for your company, but there is one counterfeit issue that you must address. It's actually a question that can make or break your business if you get it mixed up. And most people get it totally wrong.

The fake question is when you ask, "How did you find out about us?" If you have ever asked this question to a client, then you have bought into a counterfeit feedback loop.

Today's world is a constant barrage of messaging. There is absolutely no way that people will remember what impression made the difference. The choices are innumerable. Was it signage on your building or company car? Maybe a business card, social media post, or referral led the prospect to call? Or perhaps it was word-of-mouth or a billboard? People simply can't recall the precise "how."

The best question to give is, "why." Simply say, "Why did you choose us?"

Asking "why" opens up a conversation that can lead to the authentic answers you desire. There's nothing counterfeit about asking "why" your business was chosen.

The response allows you to discover what makes a difference in your marketing and community involvement.

 Tracking an advertising campaign's effectiveness by asking, "where did you learn about us or "how" did you find us will lead to skewed results. Each time your business is seen, shared, or spoken of helps. From the logo on your uniform to the magazine advertisement, each impression matters. There's not just one way that prospects decide to spend their dollars. Ask the best question of "why" for genuine insights into your business.

HOW DO YOU BUY?

It's amazing and even a little alarming that people never think about how they choose products or services. We just buy whatever we want or whatever we can't afford. The science behind that purchase is often unknown, yet it does matter, especially if you want to grow your business.

To gather attention and expand awareness of your brand, you need to stop thinking like yourself and start thinking like your customer. It doesn't matter if you read magazines, go on Facebook, clip coupons, or attend sporting events. What makes a difference for your business is being visible where your customer will see your name or logo. This is branding. Branding influences buying decisions like nothing else. What exactly is branding? Well, remember that branding is simply a marketing term for "relationships."

The brands we choose, and use are those we have a relationship with and not just the cheapest product. Coupons are great, but just consider when was the last time was you used a coupon. Have you recently told a business where you saw their ad? Why would you expect your clients to tell you where they recall your logo? Is it really the job of customers to report on your advertising efforts?

Today every purchase is a branded purchase including that can of peas from Wal-Mart or the purse from Louis Vuitton. Branding fertilizes the soil of everything else you are doing in your business. It helps the community like you and focuses on how you want to be known. Valuable branding works behind the scenes and is the silent business builder. And it functions just like how children learn multiplication. Kids see flashcard equations and memorize them to recall later. A child looks at 2x2=4 repeatedly until they know the formula by memory. The more we see an advertisement the more we recognize the brand. This is effective for kids and adults. Just take McDonald's for example.

Through time, consistency, and repetition McDonald's has become the most recognized restaurant in the world. (Even when most people don't readily admit enjoying their fried foods!) You might think McDonald's doesn't need to advertise, but they spend over 624 million dollars on ad expenditures annually. And they have done this for decades. McDonald's understands that when business is good you *should* advertise, when business is challenging you *must* advertise.

A brand is what people imagine when they think of your company. What pops into your mind when you read the word McDonald's? That is their brand. McDonald's understands that staying top of mind keeps customers returning. They have been consistent with their logo of the golden arches since the 1950s. Even toddlers recognize that simple symbol. A brand identity helps people remember your business and that takes time. In general, people need to see an ad 7 times before they will act on what they are seeing.

So, how do you buy? Or how do your customers buy? That answer is simple – we all buy brands.

YOU'VE GOT A MINUTE TO WIN IT

Minute to Win It is a game show where contestants compete in 60-second challenges with everyday objects often found around the home. It's a fun reminder of the power that can be harnessed in a few seconds. If you only had one minute to explain your business to someone, could you do it effectively and memorably? Having a quick spiel prepared will help you maximize many conversations.

Why would people choose you? When you share, talk about the benefits of your business and not just what you do. Explain how the problems you solve or the services you offer bring the client value. Accentuate those! Instead of saying, "I own a restaurant," you could proudly proclaim, "I create lasting memories through great-tasting meals" or "I make people fat and happy with burgers and fries." If your intro is catchy or funny, it will also grab attention. Using words, pictures or humor in your pitch helps people be open to lean in to learn more.

Keep your talk conversational. Don't talk "at" people. Talk "to" them. Nobody wants a speech. Engage in a short conversation to connect and communicate about yourself.

You could also talk about what makes you an expert in your field. Your "elevator pitch" gives reasons for people to connect with you or consider you above the competition. What sets you apart in your industry? Mention a specific story or testimonial.

In the book *Someday is Not a Day of the Week*, the author says your pitch should be short, simple, and pass the eyebrow test. "If what you say in your elevator pitch causes the listener's eyebrows to go up, you've got 'em! You've left the listener wanting more, and that's precisely what you want to accomplish," wrote Sam Horn.

You've got a minute to win it when you are in line at the grocery store, networking event, social gathering, Chamber ribbon cutting, or kid's birthday party. Having a pitch prepared will prepare your answer when someone asks what you do for a living. Here are a few additional tips...

- Know your audience to connect with specific needs

- Start with a hook like a bold statement, funny quote or fact

- Describe with problems you solve without jargon or confusion

- Highlight what makes you unique from competition

- Tell a story or highlight notable partnerships and clients

- Practice until you can deliver it confidently and naturally

- Adapt the pitch to the context of the person you are talking with

- End with a call to action of setting up a meeting, trying a demonstration, exchanging contact information, or something specific

THE CHICKEN OR THE EGG QUESTION

That timeless question of "What came first, the chicken or the egg?" applies to marketing. Should you advertise before you are hugely profitable or try to grow a tremendous business first and then advertise? While each business' budget is different, we can learn from companies like Nike, who almost went bankrupt before they risked it all with their "Just Do It" campaign.

Nike originally catered their products towards marathon runners. That was not a winning strategy, so they put all their eggs in the advertising basket. In the late 1980s, Nike changed its approach and backed its "Just Do It" slogan with superstar athletes. This decision would either end the company by draining it financially or make it a household name. We all know how this story ends, and your account can be similar. Effective marketing can make an enormous difference to your company's reputation and, eventually, bottom line. Profitability comes after your target market knows and uses your services.

The U.S. Small Business Administration website suggests that up to 20 percent of gross sales be allocated to marketing. "This budget should be split between

1) brand development costs (which includes all the channels you use to promote your brand such as your website, blogs, sales collateral, etc.), and

2) the costs of promoting your business (campaigns, advertising, events, etc.). Whether you run a small business or a multi-million-dollar corporation, marketing is essential to your profitability and growth. Yet many small businesses do not

allocate enough money to marketing or, worse, spend it haphazardly," wrote Caron Beesley for the USBA.

Yes, it is often hard to plan money on ads that you can't track or know if there is a return from the spending. Marketing is an investment in your business's future and must be part of your budget like payroll or rent. It may be one of the few budgetary line items that is both a tax write off and advancement of profitability. Because it allows you to speak directly to the consciousness of the community, it seems that the chicken of branding comes before the egg of success.

Marketing matters because it increases your brand's awareness, need, and desire. With adequate advertising, you can become a household name like Nike. Without it, you can have the best service at an amazing price and still struggle to gain market share. Learn from Nike and run towards branding.

A Different Direction

One company took a different direction with marketing to appeal towards a specific small audience to create and retain loyal customers. 5-Hour Energy didn't just run commercials on every media type or spend millions in ad buys online. Instead, they did smart sponsorship, and that's something your company can do – regardless of your size or budget. Here's their story and how it worked.

At the company's launch, it was unheard of. 5-Hour Energy knew it needed a powerful engine to promote its brand. With so many options, they did something unexpected. They partnered with NASCAR, one of the most potent branding mediums, to establish long-term trust. NASCAR allows companies to sponsor vehicles or teams, which builds a loyal following over time. Teams are named after businesses, and that name is repeated over and over. People feel good about the team and then feel good about the company. 5-Hour Energy sponsored a vehicle, and people slowly began choosing the energy shot drink. This took time. They couldn't sponsor a vehicle for one lap, one race, or one season. Instead, 5-Hour Energy trusted a multiple-year campaign to bring results over time. In fact, it is said that NASCAR came right out and said, "Don't expect any results right away. You're not going to get anything in the first several months. Later, you will."

Indeed 5-Hour Energy was nervous after not seeing a direct response immediately. Months passed, and nothing happened. Then slowly, things began to change. Their sales began to grow, and they turned into a billion-dollar company. Now, 5-Hour Energy sponsors a professional golfer and other sporting teams.

It takes time to build awareness and likeability, which is why repeated messaging is so important. When your company brands, the most crucial ingredient is frequency and consistency. Short-term, one-hit wonders don't work. Sponsorship of a cause, advertising medium, event, or non-profit connects your business emotionally in a powerful way. Sponsorship aligns you with the community and compellingly gives exposure. 5-Hour Energy discovered this and so can you.

Here are a few additional ideas for local sponsorship:

- Local sports teams like youth or adults

- Community events like festivals or cultural events

- School programs and scholarships

- Local charity or nonprofit organizations

- Art exhibitions, music concerts or local theater

- Community festivals or farmers' markets where you can set up a booth

- Business associations like the chamber or industry-specific groups

- Adopt-a-highway, tree-planting, community cleanups

- Youth programs or clubs

- Health fairs or wellness events like charity runs or fitness clubs

- Local media sponsorship with radio, newspapers, magazines, podcasts, and other platforms that are dedicated to local stories

YOU CAN UNLOCK EFFORTLESS MARKETING

Advertising is more challenging than it used to be. Years ago, spreading your company's name was easy as in most areas there were only a few television or radio channels, a local newspaper, and maybe a billboard. The world has changed, and today's consumers are aghast with various media. These multiple methods of marketing actually hurt your advertising efforts. You can't be everywhere at once, reaching all people, without investing tons of dollars. Options like streaming television, satellite radio, temperamental social media and the internet leave the market diluted and challenging to reach. Here are four easy ways to advertise effectively:

1) Engage the community through networking at the local chamber or other groups. Being visible is critical to building credibility and top-of-mind awareness. Simply showing up at events reminds people of who you are and why they should choose your services or products.

2) Ask your current clients for referrals. Word of mouth is tricky because only bad news spreads like wildfire. Good news travels like a snail unless you ask satisfied customers to recommend you. Simply say, "who do you know that might benefit or like our services?"

3) You can do good and market your brand at the same time. Find a local charity or non-profit and volunteer. Wear your company uniform as you help people in need or even pick up trash on the side of the road. This also engages your employees and shows them that their job makes a

difference. One article published in the *Harvard Business Review*, titled "What Does Your Corporate Brand Stand For?" emphasizes the importance of a clear brand purpose beyond selling products or services. The article argues that a strong brand purpose can help businesses differentiate themselves from the competition, build customer loyalty, and attract and retain top talent.

4) Use homegrown media to reach hometown folks. Targeting engages the community and leaves a lasting impression so people remember you when they are in need. Unless you have a global reach or want to market to tourists, spending money on big media is often a waste, as those paid-for impressions are given to people who will never become your customer.

HOW TO STAY TOP OF MIND

Have you ever had that dreaded conversation when deciding which restaurant to choose when you are going out to eat? You ask your kids where they'd like to go for dinner, and they mention the same restaurants you always frequent. You literally pass eight other places on the way to their favorite. Now, ask yourself, "Why is that greasy place always chosen?" The answer is TOMA. What is TOMA?

With advertising, TOMA stands for "Top of Mind Awareness." It's the main reason so many buying choices are made, including choosing your last restaurant meal. Consumers gravitate toward the familiar, reliable, and trusted. When a company is top of mind, that means they are remembered in a way that attracts attention. For a company to be profitable, it must win the battle of mental competition. Out of sight is out of mind. This is proven by the world's most recognized fast-food chain – McDonald's. This classic drive-thru is popular because of its convenience and continual advertising. Most people don't readily admit they like Mickey Ds, but they frequent the golden arches because of TOMA. Even children, before the age of two, can easily recognize the Happy Meal logo.

Quick! Think of 3 different doctors or medical offices. Those you considered are probably ones that you have visited. Or perhaps you heard their recent advertisement. TOMA teaches the importance of repetition as there are literally dozens of physicians and hospitals that you didn't consider. Being top of mind is being easily recalled.

There are plenty of places where the public can spend their money, so you must give people a reason to shop with you. And you must present this reason in a compelling way, repeatedly. You've achieved top-of-mind awareness when someone thinks of an industry, and they immediately think of you. This can be accomplished through branding and sponsorship coupled with delivering quality service at a fair price. Whether you are a restaurant or service company, TOMA is the goal of marketing as it is how people pass your competitors to do business with you. No golden arches are required!

ROI: RETURN ON INVESTMENT ISN'T WHAT YOU THINK

Should advertising come with a return on investment?

This is a simple question to answer as we all expect a return on dollars spent. However, business owners don't apply this same logic to the mortgage, electricity bill, or payroll. For some reason, marketing often comes with a different expectation - if a business spends $1,000 on ads, it should get back $1,000 or more in direct return. Foolishly, people think a penny shouldn't be spent on marketing if that penny can't be tracked. Not a single business expense gives a guaranteed return! No one thinks the sewage company is failing if customers don't mention the toilet water in the store. The cost of the trash service isn't justified by customers who say they saw waste baskets being removed, so why is advertising treated this way? Why don't business owners apply ROI tracking to what they spend on toilet paper or WIFI?

The billboard, newspaper, radio, or magazine advertisement is not an ATM. You should refrain from putting money into advertising and expecting to instantly get more money out. Instead, the return on investment of marketing is awareness. And you cannot put a dollar value on awareness.

It's imperative to understand why people make buying decisions. People buy because of need, name recognition, and branding. Therefore, ROI doesn't mean "return on investment" but "recognition only intention." The only thing an effective marketing campaign can do is build awareness. A magazine ad cannot force someone to choose your company. A magazine ad can reinforce awareness, so your company floats to the top when the need arises. Awareness is what matters most!

Don't buy the lie of empty advertising promises that offer an exact return.

To know if your marketing is working, you should judge if more people know about your business than they did a year ago. A solid message repeated to the same audience enhances your brand and reputation. Again, people buy because of name recognition and branding. This is why any advertisement you run should have a simple message – the less said the more is remembered! Your marketing dollars build brand awareness, so people remember your services or store. Perception becomes a reality to your target market over time through consistent long-term branding. The return on investment for advertising is awareness— nothing more and nothing less.

USE THESE
SUPER BOWL INSIGHTS

Even without an NFL budget, you can learn advertising insights from Super Bowl sponsors. Imagine spending $6 million on one 30-second advertisement and having no trackable way to determine if it was effective. That's exactly what companies do every year during the Super Bowl. And it works! Why? Because the pigskin matchup puts eyeballs on ads. Awareness is really the only intention for Super Bowl promotions.

Such recognition is the intended desire for any type of advertising. Dollar-for-dollar return from marketing isn't imaginable for major corporations, and it shouldn't be a concern for your business either. Don't miss this Super Bowl insight – your advertising spend brings attention to your company, and that attention cannot be fully tracked.

Companies don't just advertise during the world's most-watched football game - they are active sponsors who make the game possible. Without them, the game wouldn't be played. They know that sponsorship is an effective method to connect emotionally. Sponsorship says, "I care" in a remarkable way. Industry leaders like Apple and Nissan understand that buyers transfer feelings from the place an advertisement is viewed to the product promoted. And that's the point of branding - to create desire, knowledge, story, and worth. Sponsorship is an effective and remarkable way to do this!

Super Bowl commercials work because they are compelling or entertaining. They capture attention and strike a nerve to tap into the viewers' emotions. They are also concise. Notice how only one idea is expressed in that short half-a-minute spot. During that quick exposure, keywords are utilized to build recognition and aid memory. This is often contrary to local businesses that try to cram too much information into advertisements. Often, more can be said with less.

It's also interesting that none of the companies seen during the Super Bowl actually "need" to advertise. They already have enough business. Insurance agencies and Doritos chips choose to spend millions to be top of mind and lock out their competition. That's something else important when it comes to running campaigns. Marketing in print, digital, or on the air sends a message of success. When your ad is seen, it indicates market share and trustworthiness. The size of the ad or even the fact you are investing money in marketing indicates you are successful and viable. Not advertising removes any chance that people will remember or admire your brand.

Yes, Super Bowl commercials are often more memorable than the game or halftime show. These TV spots connect with the audience without the traditional flair of direct-response advertising. Billion-dollar companies have one chance to leave an impression and not waste a single syllable on coupons or offers. They often make their advertisement about the client and about what the company stands for instead of discounts. They emotionally relate to the audience through sponsorship with a compelling singular message. This is in stark contrast to how small and medium-sized companies typically market.

These lessons from the Super Bowl can be learned and applied for better business results and your own wins!

BETTER THAN WONKA'S GOLDEN TICKET

A golden ticket was the desire of every child and adult in the fantasy book *Willy Wonka & Chocolate Factory*. This ticket would be a dream come true as it gives access to the world's most incredible candy store and unlimited sweets for life. Too bad there's not a golden ticket to track advertising. Nope, it is totally impossible to trace the origin of every transaction.

Consumers don't always remember "where" they saw your logo. Most ads point people to Facebook or Google; therefore, these online avenues seem to generate the response. Who remembers where they first tasted milk chocolate? Can you recall the first place you saw an ad for Hershey's chocolate?

The truth is that each type of marketing places your name before clients and can therefore affect a buying decision. What works is staying top of mind to your target market. Visibility to a qualified prospect will grow your business - even if you can't pinpoint how the customer found you.

Recently, Proctor & Gamble, a company that spends more money on advertising than almost any other business, hired several firms to review their publicizing. Proctor & Gamble wanted to know where their billions received the greatest return. The results were stunning. Why? Because they were inconsistent. Not a single medium of marketing commanded most of the attention. The findings were unreliable and unpredictable. The firms were left with one primary piece of information: "We're not sure. It must all work. A mixture of marketing is effective.

Purchases can't be traced to an advertising origin." What matters is that they promoted their products.

 This huge company, with unfathomable resources, struggled to determine the "best" type of advertising because it all matters. Each touch counts. That sponsorship is seen. Your logo being visible works. Referrals help. Having a dependable product or service is important, too!

 Asking a client "where" the heard about you only gives false information. People don't remember the exactness of marketing. They never have. Years ago, folks would answer with the "Yellow Pages" and today people answer with "Google." The search engine, like the phone book, is only a listing of companies. And its that list that is often attributed.

 Trying to track the direct response of advertising is futile. Like those searching for Wonka's golden ticket, likely, searching will only bring frustration. What specific type of marketing works? Well, it all matters.

5 SURPRISING REASONS TO ADVERTISE

Why spend money on advertising if you have a sign, are well-known, are already busy, struggling for business, or just opened?

If business is good, it can be hard to justify spending dollars to find new clients - why waste the money? And if the business is slowly drying up or your company is new, spending money on marketing that might not work effectively is often difficult. Placing your business before the community is vital for any company of any size. Here are five proven reasons to market regularly.

1. **Marketing creates top-of-mind awareness.** Professional brand recognition must be a priority, so people think of you when they need you. If you aren't advertising, you leave room for competition to take up that space. Don't get lost in the noise of life!

2. **Advertising keeps your current clients loyal.** Marketing is not just for new business! Share new products or enhancements with existing customers to grow your bottom line. By reminding your past and current customers you are still out there, they can use you and refer you to their friends. Again, marketing also keeps your competition away. It protects your existing customers from going elsewhere.

3. **Content creates long-term relationships.** Trust grows as you provide information about your industry, so people recognize you as an expert. Don't tell people how great you are - show them helpful content like blog

posts, photos, videos, and other means. Content is king because it places your thoughts in the public's minds.

4. **Sponsorship is a way to connect gently with buyers.** Your support of that local sport or church tells people you care. It endears your business to the community in a gentle way. When you give back, it shows that you are more than just a cash register because you are interested in helping others. Smart sponsorship supports neighborhoods, teams, schools, or causes that matter to you. Sponsorship allows pennies spent with you to be funneled to important causes.

5. **Branding does attract new clients over time.** If done right, you can magnetically pull those with a deep pocketbook to your business. Placing your name or logo consistently before an audience creates a strong desire for your services. The more you are seen, the more you are remembered. Wealthy eyeballs continually on your ad have people salivating for your services.

HOW TO USE EVENTS TO GENERATE PUBLICITY

Everyone loves a Fourth of July cookout or a stroll at a local festival. These events create lasting memories that leave a smile on your face and a desire to return. You can create similar events for your business, with or without a storefront.

Events give people something to talk about for days to come. If they are held properly, they can create good word-of-mouth discussions that can help future sales. Hosting an event generates good awareness and even a fear of missing out for those who might be unable to attend.

Where to start with an event? Well, leverage an upcoming holiday or create your own reason to celebrate. For example, if your company has a new product or service, you could create a VIP guest list and invite people to learn about the offering. Create a personal invitation with a lovely hand-written note, phone call, or request. Or hello... there are holidays every month that can be celebrated!

Most networking groups or chambers of commerce will hold a ribbon cutting when you are opening, expanding, or marking an anniversary. The chamber will help promote this time, which marks your growth in the community. Whatever the occasion, invite your friends, family, customers, and local dignitaries to attend and party with you. You can also partner with other local companies to provide door prizes, catering, or swag bags. Plan ahead and spread the word!

Holidays indeed provide opportunities to host get-togethers. You can take advantage of July 4th or Groundhog Day to give back to your customers. Offer a sale on specific items on different days of the week. Use those special times on the calendar to show appreciation with a drop-in or party. A few decorations and simple refreshments go a long way. A fundraiser for a local non-profit, like a food or blood drive, partners your clients with a cause that matters.

Events help build brand awareness and interact with customers in a unique way. They even energize your employees and customers with excitement. That parking lot party or Halloween costume contest also gets people posting on social media. As a business owner, you should always think of ways to promote your company, so your brand is in the spotlight. Hosting a highly anticipated event is a way to do just that as you have fun and generate publicity. So go ahead and party on!

UNLEASH AND UNDERSTAND THE 95/5 RULE

Ugh. Can you feel the frustration? The annoyance and irritation are real. No business owner feels good when they write a check for advertising. That bank draft for marketing can seem like a waste of money. Why pay for something that may or may not work? The answer to these business blues is the 95/5 rule.

The 95/5 rule of business explains how 95% of marketing is seen by a client before they are in the market for the product. Yes! You read that correctly. 95% of advertising will not lead to a "response" anytime soon. Most of your marketing reaches people who are not even thinking about you, your business, or your services. Ouch! The Ehrenberg-Bass Institute conducted a study that shows only 5% of buyers are in the market to purchase... anything right now. The majority of people who will experience your ad can't and won't be persuaded to jump on an offer. Those who expect to have significant sales within weeks or months of starting a marketing campaign are surely going to be disappointed. Advertising raises awareness but it cannot create the need for a service.

Even the best commercials, with the hottest stars and the most fantastic offers, cannot guarantee results. Because this is true, it is really difficult to define if an ad campaign is "working." With the knowledge of the 95/5 rule, it is clear that it is virtually impossible to determine if a billboard or display ad "works" to build business. Marketing is not a magical ATM where you place $1,000 in for and are guaranteed to get back $1,000 or more. Sadly, many business operators have this unrealistic expectation for unrealistic results.

For example, every commercial for an injury attorney, no matter how cringe-worthy, raises awareness of the lawyer and the basic idea of legal services. That ad plants a seed - it can't force someone to call the number on the sign. Is it the job of the billboard company to cause physical pain so people call that ambulance chasing attorney? Of course not. Is it the job of the road builder to ensure a car is running smoothly? No. Those working to pave the interstate don't ask about oil changes or air conditioner filters. Their job is simply to make a great road. Those who sell advertising do just that – they sell access to their platform. It's not a marketing agency's responsibility to literally change buying habits.

Think about it. If grandma dies, the family will not turn to the latest newspaper to find the display advertisement for the phone number to the funeral home. Or people don't scan radio stations for contact information of plumbers when a toilet explodes and dirty water is spewing everywhere. When a need arises people often Google search for companies they recognize (from previous advertising) and then choose who to use. All marketing points to that last step of search!

Frustration is sure to set in if a business owner pays for advertising with the expectation of an immediate or even imminent dollar-for-dollar return. That's just not how branding works. Instead, the business owner should use a creative way to be remembered by future buyers. Top-of-mind awareness places your solution in the forefront so when someone is interested, they will seek you out automatically. It will just happen. Advertising expectations should be aligned with long-term results. Remember the 95/5 rule when planning and paying for your marketing.

IS YOUR NETWORKING NOT WORKING?

Ever feel butterflies in your stomach before attending a networking event? Or do you think those hours are a waste of time? If networking isn't working for you, consider a few tips on how to get more from those meetings.

First, take a deep breath and realize that most people aren't 100% comfortable walking into a room of strangers or business executives. You aren't alone in that struggle! Showing up is the initial step. The more you have a presence in the community, the more people will recognize you. Connections can only happen if you attend.

Have a purpose for your attendance. Before going to that ribbon-cutting or luncheon, decide on the intention for your time. Go into the event determined to meet a specific person or business leader. Set a goal and push yourself to accomplish it, even though the awkwardness. Gather cards from folks to follow up with later. Giving a call, email, or sending a note after meeting someone can make a lasting impression!

To make the event more comfortable, meet up with a partner or friend and go together to introduce yourselves to people you might not know. As you chat, show good body language by opening your posture and not blocking people out. Have a firm handshake or a nice fist bump! Eye contact is vital, too. Don't sit in a corner or even sit at a table waiting for the event to start. Stand and share with others. Network in the room - that's why you are there, right?

Keep in mind that networking groups were not created to be the main source of immediate sales. You shouldn't just seek to "sell to the room." These organizations are there to allow members to capitalize on the networks of others. Success with networking is not about the specific person but who they know.

It is human nature to forget names, so remember to wear a nametag. This removes that awkward feeling of asking for a name when you know you should remember it. It even encourages people to walk up to you as the tag makes it more comfortable to say "hello." Wear your name tag over your heart so that it is easily visible when you shake hands.

Yes, making small talk or waiting around for an event to start can sometimes feel odd. You can get more from meetings by being mindful of your actions. You can get better at networking and making an excellent impression to benefit your business. Use these tips to make small adjustments for a large payoff from your networking time.

LESSONS FROM A CUP OF COFFEE

What can a cup of coffee teach you about marketing and business? Here are a few of the many lessons to learn from some java...

Have you ever noticed how each coffee shop has its brand and unique offering? Branding causes you to pay $7 for a venti when a gas station coffee is just a buck. People pay for the logo and experience - not just the flavor. There are coffee snobs who will only drink their favorite. Similarly, you can create a brand snob who refuses to do business with anyone but you!

It's easy to connect over coffee. Invite a customer, vendor, or another business leader for a breakfast blend. Get to know that person by letting them talk while you sip. Be prepared with questions about their goals, interests, and networks. Listen and learn to build a relationship. Be interested and not just interesting.

Some like bold. Others crave blonde or dark roast. Tastes differ. It's the same with marketing. You can't reach everyone all the time. So, pick a brew and go after that crew. A response from a small, targeted audience is usually larger than a pitch to the masses. Be the favorite flavor to those clients who give the greatest return.

Saying you want "just a coffee" isn't the same as asking for a "hot oat milk skinny dirty chai tea latte." When you ask for referrals, you have to be just as specific. It would be best if you mentioned the name, business, or specific industry you are targeting. Being vague will lead to vague results. Asking for referrals doesn't work for most people because they aren't direct and specific. Order your referrals just right!

The best part of waking up is... you guessed it. And you know that slogan because Folger's advertised it for many years. Your tagline is powerful when you repeat a simple message again and again. Maxwell House was the best-selling coffee for over 100 years thanks to their slogan, "good to the last drop." Your slogan is also powerful when you invest to broadcast it regularly. Advertising energizes your business like caffeine. Coffee companies take a few pennies from each dollar sold and direct it back to building their recognition. Even when their brand is well known, they keep it in front of us and top of mind. How much of your gross sales are you purposefully using for promotions?

Taste the aroma of a regular marketing plan. Coffee beans don't roast themselves; customers don't appear from anywhere. Having a growth plan that includes long-term marketing gives you peace of mind. Look for ways to be visible in your community through sponsorship and involvement. Share your company's purpose consistently like you would a tasty cup of joe.

Provide excellent service and a great product to get clients hooked on your business. With marketing and business execution, that craving for coffee can also blend with a craving for your company.

Give Your Business Wings

Red Bull is a beverage that everyone is familiar with now. But at first, Red Bull had a tiny budget, and they didn't have much name recognition. How did they grow? They used "smart sponsorship."

To expand their brand, they decided to start sponsoring events and embed themselves within specific communities. They chose and targeted a particular group of people and knew they could expand from there. Who? Red Bull went to all the extreme sporting places, skate parks and ski hills. When the greatest snowboarders and skaters came off the run, they were handed a Red Bull. Why? Because everybody would go, "Oh, they're good at skiing or skating or snowboarding, and they're drinking Red Bull. I should drink it too."

Red Bull did this until people began associating the sport with the drink. Then they sponsored certain athletes so people would see the Red Bull brand coming off the hill with the best run. That's how they embedded themselves within that community. That's how we all know Red Bull gives you wings.

Their program took off like you wouldn't believe because it was smart sponsorship. They've never moved away from sponsorships like it. They continue such marketing today and even have their own printed magazine that highlights athletes and their perky drinks. Now, soccer moms drink Red Bull, not just extreme athletes. It's penetrated everywhere thanks to sponsorships, and that's powerful.

Sponsorship makes a personal introduction of your business compellingly. If you sponsor an event at a school, the Chamber, or a little league sport then you are doing good and telling others about yourself at the same time. You are replicating the Red Bull example to gain influence, so the audience potentially turns into your client base. Use sponsorship and give your own business wings.

What Advertising Can't Do

A twelfth-century proverb tells us much about business and marketing. Indeed, there is great wisdom in the saying, "you can lead a horse to water, but you can't make it drink." Here's how this phrase applies to show us what advertising can't do...

Imagine a horseback rider who is annoyed because after riding a bit the animal should hydrate itself but doesn't. The trail has led to the bubbling brook, but the horse won't sip. That irrational frustration is shared by people who think advertising equals immediate results. The greatest coupon with the highest discounts doesn't guarantee results. Even though you may think marketing will create immediate opportunities for business, this simply isn't true. Advertising doesn't make a sale. It can't. You make the sale!

Advertising can't guarantee anything. Don't mistakenly think marketing leads to immediate and direct sales. The greatest selling campaign has huge power to influence, but it simply cannot force people to buy a product or click on a website. Regardless of what the unicorn-and-rainbows "experts" always believe about how their magic pixie dust marketing can accomplish, it can't make people do anything. So if marketing doesn't make people buy, what good is it?

Advertising influences. That's it. It builds awareness over time. Think of ads as long-term investments that pay off gradually. Keeping your logo in front of clients helps you be the choice when the need arises. Don't you want to be top of mind when someone thinks of your industry? It is not the job of the magazine, website, radio, or flyer to seal the deal with your clients. It's yours!

For any campaign to be effective, it must be paired with a viable and affordable need or want. You can have the brightest billboard or the loudest commercial, but if your product is subpar, then the ad spend does little good. Let's say your spot encourages people to call for information, but no one answers the phone or voicemail isn't set up. That's not the fault of the advertisement. Or maybe an ad drives traffic to your website, but if it's outdated and crashes, what good is that? Or a customer visits your shop because of a postcard, but the employee speaking makes a potential customer lose confidence in your business. Poor customer experiences or bad products avoid any advertising budget. Marketing doesn't make the sale! The purpose of marketing is to create awareness and make clients curious. You could even say that good marketing creates a thirst for your company, like the horse pants for water.

The thirst for your brand is what leads people to action. Effective advertising creates this desire so your product or service is actually desired, like a parched horse craving water. It places your company at the forefront. The rest is up to you! The proverb is true, "you can lead the horse to water but can't make them drink." It's also true that you can make the customer thirsty, and that's accomplished through consistent branding.

5 WAYS TO KILL YOUR BUSINESS

Here are five proven ways to kill your business and shut the doors forever. If you don't believe these dangerous practices will stop growth, then try them! But remember you have been warned about these hazards.

1. **Poor consumer insights can hurt, even when you do not realize it.** What type of experiences do your clients have? Do not answer that question with what you would LIKE them to have but be truthful with yourself. Consider buying from your business from the perspective of a customer. How is the phone answered, people greeted, or interacted with on social media? Do your clients feel valued, cared about, and connected? Would you do business with you? Pay attention to customer reviews and talk to current clients to better understand their needs and wants. Invest in advertising to keep your existing customers! Marketing money is not just for new purchases. Make sure shoppers feel valued and they will come back.

2. **Bad hiring can drain life and profit.** One bad apple can create a toxic culture at your office. Upset employees or staff with irritating attitudes will kill your company. A key for better hiring is found in your training and retention. When onboarding new team members do you have a system to help them feel welcome, competent, and cherished? Walk with your team throughout their day to really understand what happens. Be an undercover boss. Ask existing employees who love their job to help you find new employees. And ask them why they love working for you! Focus

on this when you are doing interviews. Customers will easily go online or to your competition if their experience with your staff is not pleasant. Hire slowly and fire quickly!

3. **Many companies go defunct because they do not have the proper funds that are required to keep their business updated and in the minds of clients.** When was the last time you upfitted your building? Have you purchased new products or offered new services recently? To make money you must spend money! One of the greatest places to spend money is on yourself - go to conferences and continue education in your field. And treat your staff to unexpected rewards like small gifts, a pizza party, or a paid day off. If you stop investing in your business, then your business will stop.

4. **Do not advertise.** Simply pretend everybody knows what you have to offer, and your business will go down quickly. Too many owners tell themselves they just do not have time to think about marketing or they do not have to spend money to promote their business. Some mistakenly convince themselves they have been in business so long that customers will automatically come to them. You are in the danger zone if you forget that your competition is always trying to attract your customers away from you. Do not overlook the fact that advertising is an investment in your bottom line – it is not an expense.

5. **Do it alone!** Yes, being an entrepreneur can sometimes feel like you are on an island, but you are not. There are organizations and groups that want to help you expand and succeed. Connect with these people and you will see referrals grow, profit rise, and your business explode. The local Chamber of Commerce, Small Business Development Center, networking groups like BNI, the Small Business Association, SCORE, and others are available to help you. Listen to good advice on podcasts. Read books on leadership and management. Learn from your competitors. Ask experts in your industry. Be open to learning or do it alone and close for good.

DECISIONS, DECISIONS AND DECISION FATIGUE

A little boy asks his father: "Dad, what does it mean to be a man." The father replies: "well son, being a man means that you're the person in control of the situation, you're the one who makes all the important decisions."

"Well," the kid answers "then I hope to be a great man when I grow up, just like mom is." Wouldn't it be nice to make the best choice for each important decision?

As a leader you are faced with numerous decisions every minute of every day. From product development and pricing to marketing strategies and customer service, the choices you make can have a significant impact on your business. Psychologists have discovered a phenomenon often at work behind the scenes of your brain that can affect your ability to work effectively: decision fatigue.

Decision fatigue is a psychological occurrence that manifests when a person makes a series of selections over an extended period. As a result, their ability to make sound decisions becomes impaired, leading to poor choices, indecisiveness, and procrastination. It's at work in the life of everyone everyday everywhere. It can have a significant impact on your life, affecting everything from how you run your business to how you treat your spouse. "The idea is that after making many decisions, your ability to make more and more decisions over the course of a day becomes worse," said Dr. MacLean for the American Medical Association.

We all know that the number and the weight of your choices can wear you down throughout the day. Effort is given consciously and subconsciously to everything from what shoes you are going to wear to if you will hit the gas at the yellow light.

Decision fatigue sets in as the day continues and stress mounts. One of the greatest symptoms of this syndrome is avoidance. People ignore, neglect, and put off choices when they feel drained. Have you ever felt paralyzed with a choice and responded with "I need to think about it" only to just put the decision out of mind? Many are often paralyzed by the fear of a negative incorrect selection, so people choose to shut down and avoid the issue. Worn-out brains reason that it's easier to put something off until tomorrow than to make the wrong decision today. It's hard to determine what is best for your business when you're stretched thin. And when decision fatigue occurs it only permeates the cycle.

No one would want to make a poor choice, leading to a decline in customer or employee satisfaction. And you definitely don't want to decide on a marketing program that wastes money. Don't fear the defeat of dumb decisions. There are things you can do when the brain fog or frustration sets in. Here are 5 ways to beat decision fatigue:

1) **Prioritize:** Focus on the most critical decisions and delegate smaller items to others on the team. Make tough choices and make difficult phone calls immediately in the morning. You can do hard things!

2) **Take Breaks:** Take regular breaks throughout the day to rest your mind and recharge. Who said a mid-day nap is bad?

3) **Automate:** Automate repetitive tasks and decisions, freeing up time and energy for more critical decisions. James Clear teaches that you should "do 1,000 things one time with a system instead of doing one thing 1,000 times."

4) **Simplify:** Simplify decision-making by reducing the number of options and focusing on the most important factors. Discipline distractions by setting specific times on your phone that social media can be viewed. Put up boundaries with staff and even family as to times when you can be reached.

5) **Outsource:** Give those tasks or choices that you despise to someone else. If it stresses you to do spreadsheets, then find an employee to help. Experts can provide valuable insights and work.

[49]

DON'T BE SCARED

It's thrilling to watch a scary Halloween movie. That jump scare really makes your heart race. A similar fear can overwhelmingly be felt when making decisions in marketing. Is it worth it to run that ad or sponsor a sports team? How many pennies from each dollar should be used towards marketing?

Marketing matters and should be a part of your regular business budget. The US Small Business Administration suggests investing up to 20% of gross revenue in advertising if you want your business to grow.

Did that number make you howl like a werewolf?

This guideline from the nation's leading business organization suggests spending $20,000 if your company brings in $100,000 gross. If your business does 500k, then one hundred grand is to be used towards marketing. This isn't money being spent frivolously, though. If done with intention, branding is investing in your business. It reinforces relationships, reminds people of your services, and reaches new prospect. So, one way to do this is through smart sponsorship.

Sponsorship allows you to create an emotional connection with the community. This is key - it tells people why you are special and not just about your specials.

The concept of sponsorship branding is simple and powerful. For example, billion-dollar brands place their logo on events or venues with the purpose of creating goodwill. Locally, you could donate to schools, athletic programs, or non-profits to place yourself top of mind as a company that cares. People shop with people, and we all choose to do business with companies that share our values. Branding builds awareness, educates, and establishes connections.

Don't be afraid to invest in the future of your business. The marketing you do today is for the sales you will make in the future. And while we all enjoy dark Halloween nights, to do business without advertising is like smiling in the pitch-black dark of night. You know you did it, but no one else can see it.

"Advertising is an art; stress is its greatest obstacle. Master the art of simplicity, and stress will fade away," said Sarah Brown and its true. Here are a few ideas to make marketing less scary...

- know your audience
- create a content calendar
- budget wisely
- have long-term expectations
- set clear goals
- budget wisely
- educate yourself on marketing

Without trick-or-treating, Halloween is just another day. Without advertising, your company and your future might not be sweet either.

Print & Digital are like Turkey and Dressing

Thanksgiving turkey always goes with dressing; peanut butter is perfect with jelly and print with digital marketing both work better when paired together. This isn't just a taste test - research recently proved how multiple impressions of different media types positively affect the brain.

Scientists were alarmed by their findings after having test subjects view ads in digital and physical media. Through a variety of neurological methods, including biometric measurements and eye-tracking, they discovered how print and digital are the perfect combination. Here's some of what they found when people saw similar advertisements in both formats.

- Digital ads were processed more quickly.

- Paper ads engaged viewers for more time.

- Subjects reported no preference for either medium.

- Subjects absorbed about the same amount of information from both media.

- A week later, subjects showed greater emotional response and memory for physical media ads.

- Physical ads caused more activity in brain areas associated with value and desire.

These findings probably don't surprise you. Most of us scroll right past ads on social media or minimize pop-ups before we give them a glance, but we are more retentive with printed paper. Print causes us to linger longer and "window shop" the various options on the page. It creates an emotional bond and desire that is greater than what online viewing can do. A growing body of neuroscience shows that print marketing affects us in powerful ways related to memory, recall, and enjoyment.

Researchers have discovered how the ventral striatum, the part of the brain whose activity is most predictive of future purchasing behavior, is activated more powerfully when it views a message in physical media. The brain section is then stimulated for greater memory with digital impressions. Effective print and digital ads work better if they reinforce consistent messaging. That Facebook ad, Google display, publication sponsorship, and newspaper spot combine for community recognition.

Print makes digital more successful even though excessive screen time can have a negative impact on life. One study has shown that more than half of U.S. consumers are concerned that they spend too much time on their devices and that it might be damaging to their health. This leads to people turning back to print for entertainment and information. Sure, mashed potatoes are good alone, but their taste is magnified when gravy is poured over them. It's the same with mixed media. "Because print is a highly exclusive medium, 71% believe printed news stories are more trustworthy than those found online. The same percentage believes reading their news in print provides a deeper understanding of the story," reads the report "Print and Paper in a Digital World: Key Findings from the US Survey."

To grow in today's market, companies need these two types of marketing. Print is personal, trusted, and has gravitas. Digital is in the moment and measurable. Together they are a strong partnership that is better than cranberries and Thanksgiving lunch.

5 Holiday Marketing Tips

From Black Friday to National Cookie Day, the calendar is full of reasons to market to new or existing clients. There are over 1,500 national days that can be incorporated into strategies to engage an audience and raise business awareness. You don't even need a special offer to capitalize on the holidays; all you need is a little creativity and a plan. Here are a few tips:

1) **Use a holiday as an excuse to connect with clients.** Send a greeting card to your best customers. Post on social media a highlight of how you celebrate. Be personal and make an engaging event. Offer snacks, extended hours, music, giveaways, and have a special time. Bring in a local "celebrity" to draw a crowd.

2) **Celebrate obscure holidays for a fun time.** You can find these listed on various websites. Make a big deal out of "Double Dare Day" or "National Hot Dog Day." You can even create your own holiday, like a business anniversary or an employee birthday. Stay active on social media with many posts, regardless of why you're having a party. There's nothing wrong with having a "Third Wednesday in May" promotion!

3) **Capitalize on the weekend after Thanksgiving.** This can be a fabulous time for engagement with Black Friday, Small Business Saturday, and Cyber Monday. An event or offer can do wonders when people are already out shopping. Big box stores often make it a huge weekend with a "loss leader." This is a product of service offered below cost that entices shoppers. Perhaps choose something that would make you, as a consumer, stop and pay attention. Promote this early and ask customers to help you

spread the word. But don't over-discount and lose too much money! Start planning for this in the summer.

4) **Involve your staff.** Include those who work for you when it comes to decorating or organizing events. People love to party! Decorating makes the atmosphere festive and sets the mood. Ask your employees what they suggest and how to best make it a memorable event. Even if you don't have a brick and motor location, you can still decorate your website or social media.

5) **Partner with other businesses or the chamber of commerce for greater impact.** Team up with companies that compliment yours. The more you give, the more you gain. Have displays at your office or at the location of other companies and highlight those you trust. You can even choose a charity for a food drive or invite the local blood bank to set up during your event.

Advertising Thoughts

"Advertising is totally unnecessary. Unless you hope to make money."
— Jeff I. Richards

"People spend money when and where they feel good." — Walt Disney

"Half the money I spend on advertising is wasted; the trouble is,
I don't know which half." — John Wanamaker

"Early to bed, early to rise, work like hell, and advertise." — Ted Turner

"In our factory, we make lipstick. In our advertising, we sell hope."
— Peter Nivio Zarlenga

"Nothing except the mint can make money without advertising."
— Thomas Babington Macaulay

"Many a small thing has been made large by the right kind of advertising."
— Mark Twain

"There's an ad for every vice. That's advice." – Brian Spellman

"A brand for a company is like a reputation for a person.
You earn reputation by trying to do hard things well." – Jeff Bezos

"Brands should think of themselves not as storytellers but story builders.
We plant seeds of content and let our community build on it." – Amy Pascal

"Marketing is no longer about the stuff that you make but
about the stories you tell." – Seth Godin

"The best marketing strategy ever: CARE." – Gary Vaynerchuk

"Nobody counts the number of ads you run;
they just remember the impression you make." – Bill Bernbach

"Make it simple. Make it memorable. Make it inviting to look at." – Leo Burnett

"Content is king, but marketing is queen, and runs the household."
– Gary Vaynerchuk

"Stopping advertising to save money is like stopping your watch to save time."
– Henry Ford

"Don't tell me how good you make it; tell me how good it makes me when I use it."
– Leo Burnett

"The difference between the almost right word and the right word is the difference between the lightning bug and the lightning." – Mark Twain

"Doing business without advertising is like winking at a girl in the dark.
You know what you are doing, but nobody else does." – Steuart Henderson Britt

"Telling lies does not work in advertising." – Tim Bell

"People don't buy what you do, they buy why you do it." – Simon Sinek

"Facts are irrelevant. What matters is what the consumer believes." – Seth Godin

"If you want to understand how a lion hunts, don't go to the zoo.
Go to the jungle." – Jim Stengel

"The advertisement is the most truthful part of a newspaper." – Thomas Jefferson

"If dogs don't like your dog food, the packaging doesn't matter." – Stephen Denny

"All you have in business is your reputation –
so it's very important that you keep your word." – Richard Branson

HAVE CLIENTS
SING-ALONG WITH YOU

Whether it's traditional carols or the classic Mariah Carey anthem that is played every hour on the hour in December, holiday music is meaningful and memorable. From these Christmas choruses, we can discover a great deal about marketing and especially about the power of repetition.

We learned the words of "White Christmas" thanks to joining along with Bing Crosby and others. The tune of "Silent Night" flows naturally because of years of singing during winter. All the words to these beloved carols are in our heads so we can't even be fooled with a kid singing "Batman smells" instead of "jingle bells." Repetition sears a song, a catchphrase, and even a logo into the brain so it is recalled without effort. Quick! Can't you remember the melody of "Santa Claus is Coming to Town" when you simply read that song's title? By the way, the visual of Santa with rosy cheeks, a red outfit, and a big belly is brought to you by yearly marketing and repetition (originally by the Coca-Cola company).

Repetition is used in advertising to keep a brand or product in the forefront of consumers' minds. Repetition can build brand familiarity and feeling over time. The more your logo is seen, the more it is known and trusted. Therefore, a short-term campaign or even quarterly advertising doesn't work very well. One radio spot for thirty seconds in the middle of the night isn't enough. A billboard that flashes once a month isn't noticed either. Long-term reverberation is the only way to break through the noise of the world and garner attention. This isn't just an opinion – it's a proven fact. A University of Wyoming research paper found that ads with high rates of repetition tended to also be rated as high quality in Consumer Reports magazine. A later study, published in the *Journal of Consumer Research*, confirmed that consumers tended to think products advertised with repetition were good buys. Hark! Consumers can be convinced by repetition. You wouldn't change the words of "O Holy Night" so don't change the words of your marketing message. Having a consistent brand with a slogan, colors, and layout will help potential customers and consistent clients sing along with your company.

Here's a marketing tip that can be used during the yuletide and all year long - determine a message about your company, pair it with a compelling visual image, and then keep it before your target audience without change. Know that simple and brief is easily remembered. And remember that the more information included in your ad means, the less is remembered. Researchers have often found that all buying decisions are visual – you either see something with your eyes or your ears "see" it with the description. Memorable imagery seen repeatedly is like hearing the song "Rudolf the Red-Nosed Reindeer" and visualizing the characters in your mind's eye.

We didn't have to learn to sing Christmas carols - we just sang them. With effective marketing, consumers don't have to learn to trust a company - it just happens. Trust is built with consistent repetition. And even though Christmas songs are seasonal, they are immersive. Everyone knows and can relate to them with joy. Marketing must be the same way if it will accomplish your goals - then every day can be the most wonderful time of the year!

IF IT BLEEDS IT LEADS

There's an old saying in the news business that "if it bleeds, it leads." Basically, this psychological trap explains that bad news grabs the headlines and gains attention quicker than something uplifting. The negativity and fear that is found online on television, and on the radio is there to keep you scared. Why? Well, if you are full of worry, then you will keep coming back to that media for more information. That's the news cycle: here's some scary bad news – tune in later for more things to make you worry. Is this type of traditional media where you want your business to be associated with?

Headlines and outlandish claims about a possible pandemic, world wars, or doomsday financial predictions are commonplace, even on trusted networks. This worry can easily creep into your business. What should you do if some of these claims do come true? How should your company respond if lockdowns happen or if customers stop coming?

First, it's important to remember that things are never as bad as they seem. Thinking about the worst-case scenario can affect your mental health and emotional wellbeing. Constant exposure to stories involving tragedy or crisis can lead to feeling helpless. Have you ever made a good business decision based on bad news you saw on television? Probably not.

Heightened anxiety and fear doesn't help employees feel safe or valued. If a manager is constantly complaining, then that frustration flows to the team members and clients. Consuming a disproportionate amount of news can distort your perception of the world. It can also affect your sleep, attitude, and relationships. It's easy to be irritable or withdrawn when everything seems to be in a downward spiral.

The opposite is also true. Positivity begets more positivity. This works with marketing as well. You can shape how prospects perceive your brand with memorable impressions and by placing your ads near positive, family-friendly content. When consumers associate a brand with positive imagery, they are more likely to develop loyalty and trust. These emotions foster a sense of camaraderie and shared values. This is great for word-of-mouth. Organic growth occurs as experiences are shared. Positiveness resonates well with consumers who appreciate uplifting messages and joy. Plus, if you want employee morale to be boosted then cut off the negativity and be encouraging. A staff that feels proud of their employment will be more productive.

Yes, it's important to stay informed about current events. Balance is key and can contribute to a healthier lifestyle. Doom and gloom may be all around in the news, but that isn't really news. We all know bad things happen. The world will always have troubles. You didn't start your company to close down. Don't let the negativity in the news prevent you from growing.

WORK ON IT AND NOT IN IT

The new year is a perfect opportunity to stop working IN your business and to work ON your business. There is a difference. One of the most impactful ways to work ON your business is to focus on your future. Here are a few ideas to have a vision for your future:

Consider - when is the last time you just dreamed about what you could do, be, or have? Just a few minutes of intentional envisioning can transform your culture and profits. You probably did this when you first accepted your job or started your company. The cobwebs of complacency can easily set in and cause the status quo to be accepted. Dust off those dreams and rekindle your passion. Think again about the possibilities for your company or career. What amazing things can you accomplish? How big can you grow? Which organizations can you partner with to impact the community? If you can see it in your mind, then you can experience it in your world. One proven tool is a vision or dream board where you can foresee and predict your future. How about creating a vision board for your company? "If you want to reach a goal, you must see the reaching in your own mind before you actually arrive at your goal," said Zig Ziglar.

Having a vision for your business can make your dreams a reality. This isn't the idea of setting goals for sales or earnings. That can come later. Envisioning your success can transform your year. A dream or vision board is a poster or even one page that gives a tangible example of your desires. Here, pictures and words display goals and lofty aspirations of that expansion, profit margin, dream vacation, career goals, or finances. There is nothing magical about a dream board, though!

[63]

Creating a panel of all the things you want your company to do simply places these ideas before you. They are in your line of sight – thus the name "vision board." Simple and small choices can compound to help you reach all you ever wanted. Success takes one step and one day at a time. With a goal board it is much easier to make wise choices that support your hopes because you have created a visible reflection of your ideal outcome. So, go ahead and dream a little!

Visualization works. Scientists have tested its power and in a recent study, *Psychology Today* reported that the same brain patterns are activated when a weightlifter lifts heavy amounts or if they just imagine or visualize lifting the weights. Your board can have the same power over your business and your personal life. If money or time were not a hindrance, where would you want to live, what would you like to accomplish, how many people would you like to employ? Which groups would you support or what type of growth can you envision? Think about these questions and then put pen to paper. Dreams lead to goals, which can be broken down into steps, producing results. Visualize success and your vision board coming true. Take a few minutes each day to feel "as if" and you will experience abundance.

You work IN your business every day as you oversee your staff or help clients. Work ON your business and you'll find your dreams come true. "If you limit your choices only to what seems possible or reasonable, you disconnect yourself from what you truly want, and all that is left is a compromise," wrote Robert Fritz.

When Should You Advertise?

The most crucial question a fiancé will ever ask is, "will you marry me?" The most impactful question a business owner will ever ask is, "when should I advertise?"

When should a company advertise? Well, if you want to grow profits and awareness, the answer to that question is "yesterday." The marketing you are doing today is for the business you hope to have in the next three to six months. Maybe "now" is the time you should start?

You might be thinking – "I don't need to advertise as I have enough business, and everyone knows what I do." This short-sighted thinking is detrimental to business growth. Success today doesn't guarantee things will continue. There are always competing companies that could steal your client base. The economy has its swings. Bad things can happen overnight. You must do something to market your business continually, even if everyone within a 10-mile radius knows about your company and even if you are slammed with work and booking jobs into next year.

Advertising, regardless of medium, takes time to execute properly. There are no magic bullets that work overnight. The purpose of any marketing is to make impressions, so the audience recognizes your brand. This happens only after multiple exposures.

When you need to advertise, it is probably too late. The days of direct response are pretty much over. People just don't say, "I saw your ad" anymore. Yes, promotional or holiday marketing is important (especially if you are in retail), but this isn't the best way to invest in advertising. Branding is being remembered, and that doesn't happen overnight.

As a marriage takes time to build, branding takes time to grow in effectiveness. Year-round marketing keeps you top of mind, even if your business is seasonal. Don't you want people to think about your services before they need you, so they use you when the need arises? Branding isn't seasonal; it works continually. Even a pest control company that specializes in removing mosquitos should promote themselves during the "off season" so they can be thought of during the sunny "bug season."

Too many companies go out of business because they wait until desperate times and then try to market. If business is slower than you'd like, then a targeted campaign might be a good idea. How would you describe your ideal client? That's who you should target with your marketing dollars. Concentrate on your perfect customer and then reach them consistently in a format that gains their attention and connects you together. If profits are not where you'd like them to be, then now is the time to market more. This is a key point to consider. Never cut your ad spend! If business is slow then you should be advertising MORE to address that concern and build recognition of your brand. No business, in the history of commerce, has ever improved by marketing less. Your budget for branding should be the absolute last item you ever suggest slashing.

Like the engagement proposal, the question of marketing engagement can lead to happily ever after, or it could lead to a breakup. Advertise when you don't need to so you will never have to.

DEfiNE YOUR BRAND TO GROW

Do you reach for Chapstick or lip balm?

Do you get on webinars or on a Zoom?

Do you throw a Frisbee or a plastic disc?

Do you cook in a Crock Pot or a slow cooker?

Branding is the reason people universally call small plastic bags "Ziplock," and we all ask for a "Kleenex" instead of just a paper tissue. These products are now synonymous with their brand. Wow! That is the power of marketing. However, a well-defined brand isn't just the result of billions of dollars of advertising. It happens through intentionally placing yourself before your ideal market consistently. "A brand is a voice, and a product is a souvenir," said Lisa Gansky.

We all know, choose, and use recognized brands each and every day. These companies weren't built by accident. They took specific steps to gain and keep your attention. A clear brand is powerful to communicate to your current customers and potential clients what you do and why. *The Harvard Business Review* emphasizes the importance of building a strong brand that goes beyond just selling products or services and creates value for customers through a clear brand purpose. This idea is to focus on delivering functional, emotional, and social benefits. By investing in brand building, businesses can differentiate themselves from the competition, build customer loyalty, and drive higher business performance.

It's been said that a brand is a set of expectations, memories, stories, and relationships that, taken together, account for a consumer's decision to choose one product or service over another. Is your brand defined and known by your staff and customers? Answer these questions to build your brand so that people automatically think of you when they need your services:

- What is your brand? How do you want to be remembered? What impression would you like to leave with the public?

- Do you have a mission statement? How is this reinforced in your daily business?

- What do you do? What services do you offer? What products do you market?

- Why do you do it? What is your higher purpose?

- How do you do it? How do you serve the community? Do you have across-the-board recognition from signage to packaging? Does this match how your staff answers the phone or dresses?

- What colors and logos define your company? How consistent is your marketing with these specific elements?

- Do you know your target audience? How do you describe your perfect customer? Which demographic do you want to serve? What is your content plan to reach these people? What media works for those age groups and clients?

- What key performance indicators are you hoping to reach with your company? Which numbers matter for your success?

Who Am I?
A Success Story

Even if you don't recognize the name of Kevin Plank, you surely know his brand. And there are a few reasons why. Years ago, Kevin was selling flowers on the street while attending college. He did this simply to stay in school and have food to eat. After graduating, he lived with his grandmother as he was totally broke. He couldn't even afford to rent a one-bedroom apartment. He asked his grandmother if he could use her garage for a business idea, and she agreed. He wanted to make a jersey that would absorb sweat. She thought it was crazy but gave him the space.

To raise capital to start the business and to make the prototypes, Kevin maxed out his credit cards. He overspent on his grandmother's credit cards, too. Once the prototype was completed, Kevin had to make a choice. How would he market his product? He chose to use his budgeted amount of money to reach his target market in a compelling way. Kevin had one shot at pitching his creation and decided on the power of print. He purchased a few full-page ads in ESPN Sports magazine and ran them consistently. When the publications came out, the product took off with over one million dollars in sales almost instantly. Moving forward, he quickly recruited friends to help him fulfill the orders and ship the boxes. Today, Kevin has over twenty thousand employees, and the company makes over 5 billion in sales annually. His dream became a reality through grit and print. Who is this, and what is the company? Kevin Plank is the founder and CEO of Under Armor, and that is his success story.

Advertising your business in a tangible manner, like print, is one of the most powerful ways to attract readers to your product or service. Neuroscientists have discovered that print resonates because our brains register physical material as "real." When you hold a piece of paper or a magazine, that tangible item has a place and meaning in our world. Under Armor might not have become a household name if it wasn't for those magazine advertisements!

According to The Association of Print Media, magazines maintain the ability to persuade readers to act on ads and influence purchase decisions. Of course, these decisions must center upon a compelling product offering or a desired service. Kevin Plank provided a solution to a need and then trusted print to deliver his message. Advertising in print is a great way to build trust and give your business a physical presence in readers' homes, so your business thrives. Who knows, one day, the world may read your success story!

AIM FOR YOUR TARGET MARKET

Imagine Michael Jordan dribbling the basketball and then simply throwing it into the air without a target in mind. Or how about Tiger Woods not caring which direction he hits the golf ball? These ideas are crazy! It's also ridiculous if you don't have a target market identified for your advertising. Knowing your target ensures that your message lands with the right people at the right time. It gives you the best opportunity for a return on your investment. The more niche, the better! For example, if you are a home services company, you do not need to spend money when tourists see an ad. Why would a blanket mail piece to renters work if your product is perfect for homeowners?

Going to everyone is expensive, unproductive, and not generally a good idea. Targeting works like a laser and pinpoints you toward your most desirable client.

Knowing your perfect market allows you to build relationships and identify exactly where your dollars for marketing are being spent. A recent study showed that over 35 billion dollars in ad spend is wasted every year by companies that fail to engage their proper audience. Don't let this happen to you! The optimal market query must be answered, and you can define it with these easy questions:

1) Who is your perfect consumer?

2) What drives the buying decisions of your current clients?

3) Who would be repeat customers?

4) Which customers are most profitable in the long term?

5) Who can afford your services?

6) What problems does your company solve?

7) Who needs or wants your products? Where do they live?

8) How would you describe your current customer base?

9) Who do you think your business helps?

10) What is this audience interested in purchasing?

11) What age group, education level, gender, or ethnic background is best?

Imagine playing darts and hitting the bull's eye each time you throw. That is what can happen when you know whom to reach and then market to them appropriately. Different distribution systems share your message in specific ways with different groups of people.

Some give more control than others. You can't guarantee who will pick up a business card or anything simply dropped off somewhere for pick up. That method doesn't target very well. On the other hand, local radio can be designed to attract a specific market (think of how rap or country music genres appeal to particular people.) Certain age groups are more prone to use TikTok over YouTube. Different generations prefer Facebook and Twitter/X over Instagram. Ads at a school or event venue will not reach people who have never attended that location. To advertise to the masses might sound like a great idea, but it's akin to Tom Brady throwing a football and not aiming. As sports are about more than just plays or punts, business isn't just about products or services. You must know how to build your brand effectively or simply partner with a company that can help reach your ideal audience. A little research and judgment can allow you to understand your perfect client so you can promote them in a meaningful way.

18 REASONS TO JOIN A CHAMBER OF COMMERCE

Statistics from the *American Business Magazine* prove that joining a chamber of commerce is a smart and valuable decision when you see membership as a true partnership. As business partners, members can engage in the opportunities given by a chamber alliance for real rewards. Here are a few key points:

- 44% of consumers are more likely to think favorably of businesses that are members of their local chamber.

- 63% of consumers are more likely to buy products or services from companies that are members of their local chamber.

- Consumers view chamber of commerce members as trustworthy and are 12% more likely to believe their products or services are better than competitors.

These findings are reliable as they explain how partnering with a chamber has innumerable benefits. Here are 16 to consider:

1) Being a member increases visibility and gives you credibility for repeated exposure, so consumers recognize and trust your business. It can't hurt your business to join a chamber.

2) You can positively represent your industry with various sponsorship levels. The higher the sponsorship, the more exposure. The more exposure, the more business!

3) Experience the magic that happens at weekly or monthly meetings where you can network and build strong, genuine relationships. The more folks know who you are, the more likely they are to refer you to others. Collaborate during events and mixers to interact with other leaders.

4) The ability to find clients or vendors as you partner with like-minded business owners.

5) Through educational lunch and learns and events, you can learn more about many issues and organizations. Get involved with charities and partner to help those in need.

6) The professional development offered by chambers will make you a better person by sharpening your skills.

7) Membership allows you to easily be recognized as a leader and an essential contributor to the community.

8) Utilize the opportunity to leave marketing materials at the local office and have a listing on the chamber website. Some chambers promote companies on social media as well.

9) Membership opens the door for privileges to serve the community through strategic partnerships with schools, non-profits, peers, and local groups.

10) Your membership investment promotes business growth in the local area. It gives back to your community and reinforces your partnership with those people in your city.

11) The chamber advocates for members, ensuring your interests are represented so you can influence policies and governmental agencies.

12) Many chambers have meeting rooms that can be used for free or discounted rates.

13) Ribbon cuttings, grand opening celebrations, anniversaries, or special events can be planned, promoted, and celebrated with members.

14) Member-to-member discounts give purchasing power, allowing you to save money and help others save. You can share discounts with others and take advantage of them for yourself.

15) The opportunity to sponsor and attend events like golf tournaments and networking nights.

16) Chambers often provide news and updates to their members to keep them informed.

17) Direct access to government officials so you can voice your concerns and needs.

18) Many chambers offer business coaching, business planning, and even access to research and market data.

MAKE
WORD OF MOUTH
WORK

Psssssst! Did you hear the latest about...?

That's the goal of word-of-mouth marketing – to have people talk about your business. However, we all know that bad news travels like wildfire while good news flows like molasses. Making word-of-mouth marketing work is tricky, but it can be done. You just need to overcome the risk of negative feedback, a limited audience, and a lack of message control.

We all share recommendations regularly. It's normal to talk about your favorite restaurant or a repairman who did what he said. A Nielsen report indicated that 92% of consumers believe suggestions from friends and family more than just advertising alone. Together, the two are a powerful combination. When your clients tell others about your business, it's a powerful thing that builds upon the marketing you are already doing.

Essentially, word of mouth is free advertising triggered by customer experiences — and usually, it's about something that goes beyond what they expected. If you want people to brag about you then you must give them something to brag about! Trust is key when it comes to word of mouth, as you trust customers to bring you up in their daily chats. In the *International Journal of Market Research*, M. Nick Hajili wrote, "Trust significantly affects intention to buy. Therefore, trust has a significant role in commerce by directly influencing intention to buy and indirectly influencing perceived usefulness."

 The best way for word-of-mouth to be effective is to stir up the conversation and give people something positive to talk about. While you can't control the message totally, there are ways to steer the dialogue. For example, when you ask someone to share on social media about your company, make sure to be specific. Say, "Please like us online and leave some glowing feedback about your experience today." Or comment, "Please tell your friends about the deal and service you received with us." If you don't ask for referrals, they may never be given.

 By trusting the message of your brand to spread organically, you are expecting a natural referral process to occur. Who is that "golden goose" that brags about your company? Maybe make them a brand ambassador with rewards or recognition. Who are the influencers in your community? Engage them in your business in a fun way. Name a product after someone, give a prize to the person who sends you the most business, ask influencers to brag about you online, hold a VIP event for your faithful clients or team up with associated businesses to offer reciprocal rebates.

 Loyalty programs are a chance to reward faithful customers and spur conversations. How about posting a picture online of someone who redeems an incentive? Or you could have photos in your store of regular customers. Let people see who is shopping with you, and perhaps they will know that person and make a connection.

 Engaging clients allows them to become raving fans that promote your company naturally. This is different from attracting customers who are just looking to get a good deal and then bolt to the next discount. Word of mouth is free advertising that can affect your business in a compelling way as you partner with social networks and friendships. Its impact can be multiplied by a branding campaign. If you've relied on word of mouth in the past, then just imagine the growth that could occur if you paired it with an effective marketing campaign. With intention and some attention, you can make word-of-mouth work!

11 WAYS TO APPRECIATE YOUR EMPLOYEES

One of the most effective, yet overlooked, marketing methods is to appreciate and reward your staff. When your team is taken care of, they will take care of your customers. You can have the best advertising available, but if your product or service is delivered with a sour face, then it won't be received very well, and your profits will suffer.

Recent research indicates the gloomy environment of most workplaces. 82% of employees don't feel recognized by their bosses, and only 17% of workers believe managers know how to appreciate their employees. These sad numbers reveal the importance of marketing by simply treating your staff with kindness and respect.

Here are a few impactful and inexpensive ways to appreciate or think about your employees just a little more:

- Recognize staff birthdays and work anniversaries. A cake, balloons, or a small gift goes a long way! Who doesn't love to be bragged about on social media?

- Invite their spouse in for lunch on the company. Let them enjoy the meal together and don't feel like you should tag-a-long.

- How about a bouquet of flowers? Everyone enjoys beautiful daisies or sunflowers.

- Surprise a staff member with a pair of movie tickets. Then ask how the movie was. This provides some fun entertainment provided by the boss!

- Use a way for someone to take a day off with no questions asked. Create a "day pass" that can be redeemed with just a week's notice. Maybe even pay them for the day. The team will all want to have this pass!

- A new and improved job title recognizes the team and the public. Google some ideas to make your staff feel more important. Post the "promotion" on social media for extra appreciation. And don't forget new business cards!

- Dressing down doesn't cost anything but makes the workday go by faster. This incentive is fun and could be anything from blue jeans Friday to Hawaiian shirt Monday.

- An old-school but effective idea is to have an employee of the month. Feature them on your website or photo in your office.

- Give a handwritten note of gratitude and tell how their actions make you feel and the impact they have upon your business. Or leave a short post-it note with just one line of thankfulness.

- Have a conversation with the team members, discover their favorite charity, and then make a donation in their name to that non-profit.

- A funny reward is to do a "pet for a day" by having your employee bring their well-behaved puppy, hamster, or cat for the next shift.

- Hold a pizza part in the honor of someone who has been faithful.

- Have regular check-ins with the team to inquire about their job satisfaction, balance of work and home, or even constructive feedback.

Emojis and Smiles for More Sales

What one action can lead to more closed sales and more satisfied customers? Believe it or not, a simple smile can make all the difference. Researchers have proven that smiles are both contagious over the phone and in person. These smiles connect with consumers, lighten the mood, influence buying decisions, and create a better work environment. "Every time you smile at someone, it is an action of love, a gift to that person, a beautiful thing," said Mother Teresa.

A scientific study showed how emotions are communicated through smiling sounds. Smiles trigger visible changes to not only a person's face but also audible changes to the human voice. One researcher said, "When we listen to people speaking, we may be picking up on all sorts of cues, even unconsciously, which help us to interpret the speaker." Your voice and energy convey passion and conviction. There are many reasons in the world to smile!

People can actually 'hear' your smile. Turning that frown upside down makes an impact. Positive energy and excitement show that you aren't a robot just doing a job – you care! Perhaps change the way you answer the phone and say something like... "It's a great day at _____ this is _____ ." By saying it's a great day and smiling as they talk, your staff connects emotionally with the caller. This is important because most purchases are emotionally charged. We don't usually 'need' more things, but we buy them because an emotion relates to the product. Feelings are transferred with ownership, and that buying decision is often influenced by marketing. How many purchases have made because the buy made you feel a certain way? Many homes are full of retail therapy sessions!

Consider how emotional marketing starts with a smile and continues in advertisements and interactions. Emotional marketing is a process of forming relationships by provoking needs, aspirations, ego, and the client's emotional state. It is more effective than just informative ads. Think of a television commercial with a loud crying baby, and you'll understand immediately. Or picture an advertisement of smiling faces enjoying a big family meal, and you'll want to eat at that same restaurant. To connect emotionally is why dogs and babies are often featured in television commercials – you see them, and then you feel good! More than half of brand experience is based on emotions. We all have brands that we know, like, trust, and use because we have an emotional connection with the product. For example, a person who can afford any car may choose to drive a Porsche because it brings a feeling of prestige and success.

Smart marketing is all about the consumer and uses feelings to relate. This can easily be done by highlighting the higher why of your company and how it adds value more than promoting what you do. Patagonia understands this and often tells of their pledge of 1% gross sales that are given to the planet. Fans of Patagonia smile when they buy their products because they are doing good with their merchandise.

What are you doing to emotionally connect with your clients? Do your advertisements focus on the benefit and value the customer feels? Or does your marketing talk only about the basics of what you do? *The Harvard Business Review* published an article titled "The Elements of Value," which highlights the importance of creating value for customers through a strong brand. The article argues that businesses can create value for customers by delivering functional, emotional, and social benefits through their brand and provides a framework for identifying the specific elements of value that customers are looking for.

Targeting consumers with ads that reach them emotionally is engaging and effective. This starts with a simple smile, includes consistent branding, and continues with your amazing service or product. "Your smile is your logo, your personality is your business card, how you leave others feeling after having an experience with you becomes your trademark," said Jay Danzie.

FREE
ADVERTISING IDEAS

Marketing your business doesn't have to be a considerable expense. There are many ways to build awareness with little or no cost. Here are a few inexpensive ideas that can have impact:

- Wear your name tag or uniform everywhere you go in the community. This helps people associate your business with your smiling face. As you shop, volunteer, or attend events, people pair you and your brand together.

- Go online daily and comment on articles or posts. Always be positive! Tag people, organizations, and brands. Use hashtags on posts to capitalize on trends and searches. Update social media when you visit other local companies too.

- Cold call! Pick up the phone and start calling other businesses or residents. No one enjoys cold calling, but it works if you smile as you dial. Introduce yourself and see how you can be of service to others. Don't try to sell over the phone. Instead, just have a conversation.

- Start blogging. Free blogging platforms are plentiful. You know the ins and outs of your industry, and indeed there are folks who would like to learn your insights.

- Google your own business. What people find when your company is googled says a lot. Your Google Business Profile allows you to show up on maps, searches, and knowledge panels. Setting this up is easier than you might think. Google how to make your profile better.

- Look for discussions and forums related to your business or industry — your customers may even already be discussing your company online. Join the talk.

- Hold a "lunch and learn" to invite people to check out what you do. Maybe create online tutorials or product reviews. These are super engaging. Video content is dominating the internet these days. You are the expert in your industry, and you've got a lot to share.

- Attend events. Branding is all about visibility, and the only thing it often costs is your time to show up. Networking, governmental sessions, parties, and even religious gatherings are ways to connect with others and build relationships.

- People love seeing their names. An online or printed newsletter with updates is an inexpensive way to generate buzz. Highlight employees, products, and even current customers.

- Encourage clients, friends, and family to leave reviews and pass referrals. Organic recommendations can turn into closed business.

- Create a workshop or webinar that educates others. This is an excellent opportunity to engage others and be seen as an expert. Offer to be a guest speaker at community clubs or schools.

- Don't forget to claim your listings on websites like Yelp, LinkedIn, Twitter/X, TripAdvisor, Instagram, Foursquare, Yahoo, the Better Business Bureau, Next-door, Alignable, Apple Maps, and others.

Science Proves
How Print Wins

You don't have to be Einstein or Neil DeGrasse Tyson to understand some basic brain functions to better your business. Did you know that the human brain responds to various types of media differently? All marketing mediums are not created equal. Physical printed materials work for branding because of how it affects the brain. There's something to be said about the power of paper! According to several studies, print ads activate different parts of the brain, and viewing them "involves more emotional processing, which is important for memory and brand associations."

After fifteen years of collecting data points, it has become clear how print wins customers. For example, Temple University's Fox Center for Neural Decision-Making gauged how consumers respond to print versus digital or other advertisements. The results were astonishing. They found that "consumers reviewed print ads longer" and "print ads result in higher levels of recall."

According to brain activity, print is more effective in increasing value and desire, which sparks purchase interest. Print resonates because our brains register physical material as "real." When we can hold a piece of paper like a magazine, then that tangible item has a place and meaning in our world. The physical activity of reading increases neural action in the cerebellum, the hub for spatial and emotional processing.

Even the United States Postal Service Office of Inspector General commissioned a study on the effects of print and discovered how magazines, flyers, or postcards engage viewers for more time. This study observed that physical ads cause more "activity in brain areas associated with value and desire."

Paper has an emotional impact, and print produces more brain responses connected with feelings than digital, radio, or television advertising combined. When the brain has more emotional processing, the brand being marketed easily moves from short-term to long-term memory. It might not make logical sense, but the constant and dubious repetition of online ads can deduct from the trust of the company. "Print remains the most trusted source of marketing information," says a Forbes study.

Forbes wrote how neuroscience research proves that paper-based content offers special advantages in connecting with our brains. It is a scientific fact that "direct mail is easier to process mentally and tests better for brand recall." A 2009 study from Bangor University used fMRI to study the different effects of paper and digital media. They concluded that "physical material is more 'real' to the brain. It has a meaning and a place. It is better connected to memory because it engages with its spatial memory networks." This analysis also indicated how print advertisements produce 80% of consumer action over time compared to 45% for electronic ads. Effective print drives digital purchases, and the two can work in sync for brand awareness.

Print is straightforward and credible. It doesn't have unwanted pop-ups or annoying commercials that scream at a high volume. Print gives the reader the power to dig deeper or skim the page. It allows the brain to "window shop" the content while creating new neural pathways of recognition. "A Penn State study confirmed the power of print advertising by testing the memories of participants that read print and electronic advertisements. So, if you're wondering whether print is right for your business, the bottom line is that printed ads have much more influence on our buying decisions than other advertisements," wrote marketing expert Don Potochny.

BETTER BUSINESS FROM A BEER

Can you name the leading American beer?

You probably guessed Budweiser.

That beer was even renamed "America" in 2016 to garner more attention as a patriotic drink. That specific answer is permanently inscribed in your mind thanks to savvy marketing, but it is not correct. No, Budweiser isn't American, wasn't initially brewed in the United States, and its Belgium parent company Anheuser-Busch brews most of its beverages in China. Surprised? The marketing firm behind Budweiser doesn't want you tipsy on these details. It wants you to think of the King of Beers like you do apple pie. That's the power of emotional branding and hyper-local sponsorship.

Budweiser doesn't care where you saw their advertisement – all they care about is that you know their logo. They believe that this knowledge will lead to sales. Their marketing program is called 360/365, meaning that each day of the year, you will come across one of their products within 360 degrees of your presence. This is a compelling branding idea that you can incorporate into your business. You can have better business from a beer by learning from their best practices. And while they may have made mistakes with Bud Light promotions, the brand remains strong.

The public considers Budweiser as patriotic because it often appears alongside national events like the Super Bowl or World Series. Anheuser-Busch knows that pairing its product with feel-good content is powerful and effective for recognition.

And this recognition is all that matters to the company. They understand that sales follow brand remembrance and loyalty.

Where you see the ad matters as the brain connects where an image is noticed with its surroundings. Do you want your ad placed next to feel-good content or a news story about a mass shooting? In 2018, Budweiser paid millions for a Super Bowl commercial to highlight its efforts to provide water to victims of natural disasters in various parts of the country. The ad said nothing about the taste of their beer, and the ad still worked.

Budweiser has chosen to have its brand noticed repeatedly and has even targeted hyper-local audiences. This means that instead of broad commercials that are blared nationwide, they have chosen to dig down into specific markets and partner with musicians, artists, and sports teams. This type of sponsorship is influential. For example, recently, the company launched commemorative cans throughout the country. One of their tall-boy brews was released in the Detroit area in celebration of a new album from rapper Big Sean. This play for a specific target audience was tactical and local. Their president of marketing said, "We are going to be hypersensitive and insightful as to how Budweiser lives and breathes within a local market and then create a campaign surrounded by that."

The 360/365 approach works though the company doesn't track any advertising. They know that multiple exposures multiply results and build upon each other. In fact, Bud Light still accounts for almost one of every four beers consumed in the country. This is probably thanks to the fact that you have seen a Budweiser ad in the last 24 hours. Anheuser-Busch uses local messaging and methods of anything Americana to connect with beer drinkers. What they do works and can be replicated in your own company as you use sponsorship, targeted messaging, and consistent branding daily to build your business. Who knew you could learn so much from a brewski?

CHURCHILL, CAKE, AND SPAGHETTI

The iconic words of Winston Churchill still ring true - "never give up." Don't give in on your hopes, dreams, or your advertising! This may seem silly, but it's right.

Too many business owners expect immediate results with marketing. They are frustrated with a lack of short-term response and then pull the plug. Stopping advertising can destroy your business as it takes you off the market and off customers' minds. Imagine baking a cake and pulling it out of the oven with 20 minutes left to cook. Of course, you would never eat such a soupy cake concoction. Stopping a marketing plan too soon or doing short-term ads isn't effective either. A cake that doesn't settle is like a marketing program that never finishes. What a waste!

We all know and use products that have built their brand over years of marketing. Popular franchises spend hundreds of millions of dollars over many years to be remembered. If it takes such an investment on a grand scale for them, then it only makes sense that leaving a lasting impression on the local community will also require a committed investment on your part. No, you do not have to spend millions over decades, but the cost of marketing is going to be relative to your goals for company profit.

Too often, business owners want quick fixes to overcome their longtime business needs. Lasting impact and growth occur with consistent and repetitive exposure. Effective advertising campaigns are just that - programs that take time to build effectiveness.

[88]

Think about some tasty spaghetti. Cooking the pasta just right takes a certain amount of time. When the noodles are "al dente" they taste and feel the best. Chewy, firm pasta takes just a few minutes to cook exactly right. Executive chefs and grandmas know that you can even throw al dente noodles against a kitchen wall, and they will stick. Sadly, this is like how many businesses handle advertising. They do spaghetti marketing - trying different ideas and seeing if something sticks. Building your business is a long-term commitment and shouldn't be dependent upon spaghetti tactics.

It is sickening how so many business owners "try" advertising ideas and don't stick with them. Instead, they should remember how a cake settles, pasta cooks, and the words of Churchill when he said - "This is the lesson: never give in, never give in, never, never, never, never—in nothing, great or small, large, or petty—never give in except to convictions of honor and good sense. Never yield to force; never yield to the apparently overwhelming might of the enemy."

YOU CAN HAVE THE PERFECT AD

Ok, you've decided to advertise. Now comes the hard part! What should you include in your marketing materials? Content can make or break your campaign, so be extra careful to craft an advertisement that works to accomplish your goals. Bear in mind that advertising aims to increase recognition and not necessarily to make the cash register ring immediately. You can create the perfect ad with these simple ideas.

First, foremost, and maybe most important, remember the KISS method – Keep It Stupid Simple. The less you say the more that is remembered.

Think of your target audience and consider what message you would like to convey to them so that your brand is distinguished. Tailor your creative to draw that audience in and keep them coming back. Use a catchy headline in plain text to grab attention and cause readers to pause. Call out for attention.

Know what you want to say and then cut that idea back. Too many business owners think the more the ad includes, the more information people will see and remember. The human brain doesn't work this way. Less is definitely more! For recall and engagement, a best practice is to keep it short and again, simple.

Headlines matter! To stand out and be remembered, you should use something that is funny, asks a question, piques interest, makes a point, inspires, plays on words, is catchy, or gives an incentive. According to *Branding for Dummies*, some of the most effective words are "free, new, save, better, how, now, easy, guarantee, health, love, save, safety," and, most importantly, "you."

Don't use precious real estate for details that will be ignored. An email address or even a physical address is often dead space. Yes, give contact information but remember that most advertising plants seeds for future purchases. Don't crowd the reader!

Use colors and relevant images that compliment your brand story. No one will pay attention to an ad for a dentist that is a big black box that says, "insert smile here." Eyeballs will be attracted to the face of a smiling child or smiling puppy sitting in a dentist chair! Draw people in to impress your image and logo upon their memory.

Describe your benefits and not just features. Answer questions like... How can your company make life better? What makes your business different? Why would someone choose you over the competition? Who do you cater to? What do people want to know about you? Focus on those ideas and build conviction. "Sell the sizzle" – the benefits – "not the steak" – the actual product or service. Make an emotional connection. A list of services is going to be forgotten!

Intimately know your audience and relate to them. It's a different approach when marketing to bald men, young toddlers, home-bound elderly, or teens about to graduate. How can you engage your perfect client? Have fun. Be different. Make people smile. Be amusing. Point folks in a direction.

"The basic building blocks of a creative ad include a background image, illustrations or graphics, your business name and logo, any relevant contact information, body copy, a tagline, and a strong call to action," says adobe.com.

BEYOND THE LABEL TO THE "WHY"

Have you ever considered why people pay their hard-earned money for Dasani, Evian, or Aquafina water when tap water has the same ingredients? The answer isn't "quality" or "taste" – the answer is marketing! Consumers pay big for name-brand water because it has been promoted as better to possess and better to drink. Water is water unless of course that H2O happens to have a well-known label thanks to branding.

One could argue the price of water is inflated because of the different alkalinity levels, or that the product may be from a spring. Others could even say it's worth more money because reverse osmosis has done its magic. However, none of that matters if the beverage hasn't first been appropriately marketed. You could have the best tasting drink in human history but if no one knows about it then, well, no one knows about it! Branding works to create a positive "gut feeling" about a person or business. It defines what that organization wants to be known for. An easy definition of branding is simply "being remembered."

It takes time to build a brand, which is often frustrating for small business owners who want a direct response to their advertising. There are types of "buy now" marketing hacks that do appeal to penny-pinching clients. If you attract a customer with a discount, then the client may always expect a discount. You won't find the best clients in the cheapest mediums. Direct response offers a deal to "act now." Branding leads to purchases in the present and in the future by creating raving fans who are loyal to your business. Branding is like investing in the stock market for long-term tremendous growth while direct response is the day trading of advertising.

Branding works just like drinking water – behind the scenes when you don't realize it! And it can't be tracked with a return on investment. Just like Deer Park doesn't know how many bottles of water are sold from its inflated balloon in the Macy's Thanksgiving parade, you can't trace the results of branding. It brings results automatically over time, so your company is thought of well and thought of often.

Familiarity entices behavior when people are in "purchase decision mode." Consumer tests have proven that well-known products are chosen over similar unknown items more than 90% of the time. Buyers prefer recognizable brands and the only way to be remembered is through repetition. You can establish a mindset and perception of a product through reiteration.

Imagine that you have three choices for a drink – option one is a light brown bottle simply labeled "water." Option two says "Mom's Kitchen Water" on its container. Option three is well-known "Fiji" rain forest water that is sourced from an ancient artesian aquifer surrounded by dormant volcanoes, its purity is simply due to the fact that it's naturally filtered by volcanic rock. Which of these three would you want? The story-brand, design, logo, familiarity, and marketing of Fiji would probably influence your choice. You'd even pay top-dollar for the Fiji flavor.

Branding impacts buying decisions by stacking on top of the other marketing you are doing. We are all more likely to buy a product or pay for a service from a business that we are familiar with – from something as simple as bottled water to significant purchases. Business success isn't about just having the best beverage, service, or product – it's about being KNOWN to folks who need or want your offer. That's the basics of branding. And that's refreshing to know!

BIG NEWS!
HEADLINES HURT OR HELP

"You have to get a great headline to attract attention - it's about the lure - not the rod," said bestselling author, Michael Hyatt. Creating curiosity, asking a question, making an alarming statement, or using humor can make a difference.

Indeed, the first few words of a social media post, print advertisement, blog, or commercial, matter greatly as it's your quick opportunity to grab attention. Without a quirky or powerful headline, it's easy for your message to get lost in the noise of life. There are different types of headlines you can use to maximize exposure. A thought-provoking claim can get you noticed or clicks increased. A good headline prompts people to want to know more so they don't turn the dial or ignore your advertisement.

Writing a good headline might seem simple at first, but it's literally an art form. For example, that one sentence can answer questions or provoke questions depending on your text. It can reference a list, summarize benefits, or even generate fear. To get the most out of your headline, you should know your audience and thoughtfully appeal to them. Connecting with current or potential clients can be accomplished in innumerable manners with a catchy call out.

Let's say your small business sells shoes; your headlines might say:

- "Shoes On Sale"

- "Find Your Perfect Pair"

- "Shop Our Collection!"

- "Guaranteed Comfy Feeling"

- "Hassle-free Shopping and Returns"

- "Don't You Want a Pair of These?

- "9 out of 10 Feet Would Agree"

- "How Your Feet Can Feel Better"

- "Limited Availability for a Limited Time"

- "Don't Ever Buy these Shoes"

- "10 Reasons You Need Better Shoes"

- "These Boots Were Made for Walking"

- "Do Your Feet Hurt?"

- "Socks Love these Shoes"

- "Are Your Soles Achy"

- "Buy a Pair and We'll Donate a Pair"

As you can see, there are benefits to being selective and smart as a wordsmith. When thinking of your next headline, draft a memorable phrase to ensure your company is remembered! Use these ideas for more impact:

- Appeal to emotions

- Use humor

- Show off five stars or a type of recognition

- Ask a question

- Include keywords

- Give quotes or statements

- Have a testimonial approach
- Talk about offers
- Solve problems
- Make it too good to refuse
- Share a referral
- Give numbers or statistics
- Focus on benefits
- Highlight the unknown
- Create curiosity
- Use fear
- Use empathy
- Share advice
- Address a problem
- Make a "how to" statement
- Offer a list
- Hint at ways to save
- Sell outcomes instead of features
- Summarize
- Share a secret or a mistake
- Reinforce branding message

Strategies for Social Media

Thanks to social media we don't have to wait for the evening news to know what is happening in the world. Now, news is delivered instantly along with memes and cat gifs. Yes, our world has changed and your online presence matters greatly.

How would your customers describe your social media?

To have an active and successful social media presence, you need to be purposeful with your engagement. There's no such thing as an overnight internet sensation unless you remember the mayhem caused by the original video for "Baby" by Justin Bieber. The most profitable brands online have a specific plan for posts and messaging. And while you don't have the budget of those billion-dollar companies, you can develop an effective social media presence. Repetition is key! The more clients see something, the better, especially with digital. Here are a few tips to increase attention:

- Keep social media social. Stay away from controversial issues or politics. And never get involved with complaints or gossip. Don't forget that you always represent your company.

- Find one platform that fits your personality and industry, and then focus on building an audience with it instead of posting in several different places. Less is best. You can always add sites later. Each platform is different and requires different styles, sizes and postings.

- Get online for a purpose and then jump off! Schedule a time to engage on social media and use a timer. That timer will prevent you from getting lost in the maze of dancing videos and funny memes.

- To ensure people can recognize you without even thinking, you should stay consistent with brand images and colors. Use the same logo and taglines throughout the internet.

- Find a theme, like "National Donut Day" and get people to respond. Or ask a fun question like, "what's your favorite way to eat ice cream?" or "using only gifs, what hobby do you enjoy?"

- Don't take yourself too seriously – people want to know the real you without the filters or the perfect lighting. Let folks see you engaging with clients, at home, or petting your puppy.

- Watch for trends like video clips, parodies, challenges, or hashtags and use them to your advantage. Include your staff as much as possible and ask them to tag your company too!

- Immediately go online before leaving the parking lot of a local business. Leave a rave review with Yelp, Google, Facebook, or other sites.

- Use lots of photos and videos.

- Go live regularly and post often. Platforms change their algorithms frequently, and the best way to stay on top of the online feed is to remain engaged – especially with video.

- Be a good neighbor – share about other businesses, outstanding employees, local news, schools, or clients. Build others up. Make your social media more than just yourself.

- Delegate your social media to an employee or hire a company to manage the posts. Follow up to ensure it matches your vision for the business.

A DAILY PLAN FOR SOCIAL MEDIA

"There's only one thing in the world worse than being talked about, and that is not being talked about," is a quote to remember when it comes to building your business. Social media is a way to stay involved in conversations and thought of often. It can give you real-time access to potential clients and build brand fans through education, inspiration, or just being silly. Social media is important as over 75% of consumers report they go online and research a business before choosing whether to make a purchase. And while we all have networking apps on our phones, utilizing social media effectively for your business is different than just posting a funny meme.

Users of social media enjoy interacting with brands and these brands that are active can experience amazing benefits. A simple plan that is executed consistently can engage current customers and thrill potential clients. Gaining attention and building an audience with social media isn't done in a day – it is accomplished daily with a few simple actions.

It takes attention and intention to gain followers in real-time. This includes working on your part for daily and weekly postings, replies, tracking, and sharing content. For posts or videos to help your bottom line, you don't need to be overwhelmed and unsure of where to start. Just use these steps to start your strategy. Here's a simple checklist that can be utilized in less than 30 minutes a day:

Daily social media checklist

- ✓ Decide on a platform to engage your target audience

- ✓ Set aside blocked time to publish and interact online

- ✓ Identify movements, hashtags, challenges, memes, and current talking points – what's going on?

- ✓ Decide how you can incorporate current trends, holidays, and events in your posts

- ✓ Quickly reply to comments on your page and join the conversations on other pages

- ✓ Follow new followers or friends who have liked your company

- ✓ Identify top fans and tag them, post on their page, or mention them

- ✓ Encourage clients and friends to share, retweet, forward, like, follow, etc.

- ✓ Post a short video or reel highlighting something other than your company

- ✓ Upload an image about your company with content to educate or entertain – info graphics are popular

- ✓ Find content to share later and then future date it to post

- ✓ Check the social presence of influencers, competitors, and similar products

- ✓ Join a chat or group discussion and leave a meaningful reply

- ✓ Schedule posts for upcoming weeks at optimal times and days

- ✓ Share an image, article, or video from another local business or charity

- ✓ Comment on a friendly topic with a link back to your website or page

- ✓ Check mentions of yourself or your business and take necessary action

- ✓ Log out and track your time on social media – don't let it consume your hour or day

THE ART OF THE COLD CALL

"No pain, no gain" is a phrase that app ies to exercise and to business, especially if you choose to make cold calls. Cold calling is talking to someone who is not expecting the phone call. And while no one enjoys dialing a complete stranger to start a conversation, this is one of the quickest and most effective ways to make personal connections with a potential client. It costs nothing but your time to market your business over the phone! A simple dial of the digits can open doors, set appointments, and allow you to meet pretty much anyone. You can learn the art of the cold call and develop your business.

Before you pick up the phone you should determine who it is you desire to speak with and what exactly you want to say. Identify the purpose of the call – are you introducing yourself, hoping to set an appointment, thanking a customer, asking for a referral, offering an invitation, meeting new people, or following up on past conversations? Make a master list of prospects that you would like to meet before you start calling and don't stop until you've finished dialing through. Track your numbers so you know how many people you spoke with, how many dials were made, no answers, messages left, and conversations you've had that reached your desired outcome.

Having a script as a guide will help stay on track and keep the conversation flowing in the direction you intend. Don't try to sell yourself or your product over the phone. Instead, offer to set up a meeting so you can show what you have to offer. Allow your call to turn into a conversation. Relate with the other person and express genuine interest in the call.

When someone answers, you will either be talking with a gatekeeper or the exact person you would like to speak with. Be ready for either of those conversations! Connect with the person who answers and compliment them in some way. You could mention their business, website, reputation, or even their voice. A simple and sincere comment can relate you to the other person, so the call goes the way you desired. The four magic words of "how are you today" can set your voice apart as you genuinely engage the other person.

As you are talking, remember that you have reached out to have a conversation! It's a call for dialogue and not a monologue. The person who answers can help you open doors or lock them shut. Small talk is okay! Ask the person who answers to "point you in the right direction" of whom you should be calling. If the person says, "me" then jump right into the purpose of your ring. Share how you can help the other person instead of pitching your product or features. And don't sound like a robot – no one enjoys those spam auto-dialers or people that sound like a piece of sandpaper! When speaking, be your friendly self. Keep a mirror in front of you to glance periodically to ensure you smile as you dial. What should you do if the call goes to voicemail? You can always try them later or leave a simple, yet urgent message. Keep the recording short with a request to call you back, without mentioning any details of why. Then follow up later with, "I'm reaching out to see if you received my message."

Like any art, it takes time, persistence, and practice to be good at cold calling. As you are learning you should be ready for rejection. Some folks simply hate answering the phone. And others aren't always very nice when they talk with someone they don't know. Learn from being hung up on or what people say. Have call amnesia and don't allow previous callers to frustrate you. Cold calling works when you hone your skills through learning and experience.

ABUNDANCE OR LACK: IT'S YOUR CHOICE

Two shoe salespeople were sent to a third-world country to open new markets. What they found was astonishing. Three days after arriving they both called the office. One salesperson said, "I'm returning on the next flight. I can't sell shoes here. It is a disaster. Everybody goes barefoot." A few minutes later the other salesperson called the factory, telling, "This is the best opportunity ever! Absolutely glorious. The prospects are unlimited. Nobody wears shoes here!" Which do you think was better at providing solutions?

There are two ways to look at every situation. Of these two salespeople, one had an abundance mindset while the other saw only lack. It was the same scenario but two different mindsets. The opportunities for your business are no doubt identical. You might not be selling shoes, but you are wanting to be more profitable, expand or serve your clients better.

An abundance viewpoint allows you to see more; to perceive what is possible. It doesn't think of lack. This type of mentality is what leads entrepreneurs to flourish, artists to create, and leaders to lead. It is open to learning and growth. This paradigm places you in the driver's seat. It is full of inspiration and energy.

"In the fixed mindset, everything is about the outcome. If you fail—or if you're not the best—it's all been wasted. The growth mindset allows people to value what they're doing regardless of the outcome. They're tackling problems, charting new courses, and working on important issues. Maybe they haven't found the cure for cancer, but the search was deeply meaningful," continued Carol S. Dweck, "In a growth mindset, people believe that their most basic abilities can be developed through dedication and hard work—brains and talent are just the starting point. This view creates a love of learning and a resilience that is essential for great accomplishment."

 An Ivy League university study found that when people have a positive mindset, it can lead to receiving more abundance. Like a magnet, the mind powerfully attracts whatever is considered. The school's researchers concluded that when we "focus on one particular thing very intently, other possibilities that are right in front of us can go completely unnoticed. The brain can only absorb so much, so if your belief is "I can't do it" or "it's impossible" then any other thoughts contradicting that will get thrown out. Start training your mind to loosen its focus and create an expanded awareness. Ask yourself if you had all the time and money in the world and you knew you couldn't fail, what would you be doing? Questions like that will help to open your mind up to what's possible," wrote forbes.com. The lack mindset hinders growth, goals, and even raises in pay. The abundance mindset says there is more than enough to go around.

 Here's an idea. Consider the results you have at your business or home. Are there any areas of lack? If so, ask yourself, "are my thoughts based on scarcity, lack or fear?" If the answer is yes then simply ask yourself, "What can I do to shift my thoughts to abundance?" Like the two salespeople, you can choose how you view challenges. You can even choose the outcome. You can sell lots of shoes or you can give up and not sell a single pair – the choice, and the mindset is yours.

BRANDING IS LIKE...

What is branding? Well, it could be defined as "remembering" or even "relationships." Here are a few others ways to describe and understand this important idea...

Branding is like a good, reliable mutual fund. Why? Because it is an investment with a compounding effect. It offers the possibility of immediately attracting a client with any individual advertisement if they have a need at that very moment. Branding builds top-of-mind-awareness (or TOMA), so people are more inclined to remember the company when the need arises, even if the ad isn't front and center. Those with top-of-mind-awareness can become brand advocates and spread the word to others who didn't see the ad campaign. Referrals and word of mouth conversations should be attributed directly to branding as people must have something to talk about.

Branding is like Pringles chips. They use the slogan: "Once you pop, you can't stop," which hasn't changed in years. A primary requirement for effective branding is frequency. Once you start, you should continue. And continue. And continue. Branding is based on repetition. We learn things (even difficult things) by doing them repeatedly.

"You're in good hands with Allstate" has been around since 1950. Maybe you've heard it? "Don't leave home without it" has been the slogan for American Express since 1975. Once they popped, they didn't stop. And that's why you know them by heart.

Branding is like a diamond and like a sandwich. De Beers created the slogan: "A diamond is forever." Diamonds have existed for roughly 1 billion years, hence the term "forever." Like diamonds, a brand message needs to be factually consistent and remain constant for a sufficient time before branding can occur. For example, the slogan for Arby's is precise - "We have the Meat" and not "We have the Food." And the lyrics to the old song "I wish I was an Oscar Meyer wiener" has remained constant for decades. Branding reminds you of your favorite song from middle school. If the tune or lyrics changed then you could never keep up.

 If you find yourself lost and wandering the streets of a village in a foreign country and turn a corner to see a sign for McDonald's or Coca-Cola, you are likely to feel a small sense of relief. These brands are linked to your emotions, past experiences, and home. The best brands bond to an emotion. Effective marketing does the heavy lifting with an emotional appeal centered around family, community, and being neighborly. If a home is where the heart is, good branding hits home.

Branding works like snow landing on the road. When it starts to snow even a few flurries in the southern part of the United States, children begin to wonder..."will we get enough to cancel school?" They watch, wait and hope. Early snowfall hits the road and melts but slowly causes the temperature of the asphalt to drop. Once it falls low enough that the snow no longer melts, the snow piles up, and school is canceled! Similarly, branding works long before you see the results. Initially, people don't consciously notice an ad among the dozens they see daily. Nor do they typically notice the 2nd or 3rd. After time those ads accumulate, and the brand message is learned. A common error business owners make is giving up just before branding occurs.

Branding is like walking in the snow. How? Because it is a silent business builder. If you take a walk in heavy snowfall and then look back, you probably can't see where your footsteps once appeared. The snow covers the prints. The full effects of marketing your business consistently is often untraceable as well.

Branding reminds you of your favorite song from middle school. Like a tune you loved as a teen, brands we know, and love are often linked to emotions and may even trigger a mood change when we see them.

What Happened to BlackBerry & Nokia?

Chances are you probably use a phone from either Samsung or Apple. Is that right? Years ago, there were many other brands like BlackBerry , Kyocera, and the indestructible Nokia. So, what occurred? Where did the others go?

While many people have used brands like Motorola, something happened – or didn't happen – that caused certain cell phones to go the way of the dinosaur. It's not that Samsung and Apple had better operating systems. Originally, all technology in cell phones was pretty similar. Apple and Samsung did something crazy to move ahead. They invested in marketing. They didn't see advertising as an expense but a way to grow long term. They flooded every avenue possible and placed their name before the masses.

Samsung and Apple wanted to keep their logo everywhere so people would start to think they didn't have a choice. Everyone was seeing their ads and the desire for their product began to grow. People wanted an iPhone because their friends had one! The other companies pulled back from marketing because they thought everyone had heard of them. BlackBerry even believed they had the smartphone market totally full. By removing their ads, the competition allowed Samsung and Apple to overtake market share.

Fast forward a few years and we really don't have a choice. That's the power of branding. It places you head and shoulders above your competition. You hold the evidence of successful marketing in the palm of your hands.

An Ehrenberg-Bass Institute research study emphasized the importance of even low-level continuous advertising for long-term brand building. Consistency helps establish and reinforce identity. Other studies in psychology have shown that repeated exposure to a message enhances recall. The familiar prospects are with a product, the more likely they are to choose it when making a purchase.

If you don't advertise your company, then your competition will gain that space. Don't be forgotten like Blackberry. Create a branding campaign and become a household name. Don't think you have enough business and people already know your name and risk repeating what happened to Nokia.

EVERYTHING IS SALES

There were two signs that hung in the old man's office. One read, "mistakes made while you wait." The other said, "selling is like shaving - if you don't do it every day, then you're a bum." And while these plaques were humorous, they also held much wisdom. The man didn't take his mistakes too serious, but he did take his job of selling insurance very serious. He wasn't sleek or slimy like that proverbial used car liar. He was genuine and thoughtful, caring even. He considered sales as simply a conversation to solve a problem. With this idea in mind, it's easy to consider pretty much any interaction as a sales opportunity.

Yes, everything is sales! The preacher, plumber, and politician are all selling when they share why you should trust what they say. The teacher sells education, and the website sells information. It doesn't take a "sale" or exchange of money for selling to take place. Everything is sales and therefore, to get better at sales is to get better at life.

Sales is communication and that communication leads to decision-making. Authentic selling helps someone make the very best choice for everyone involved. For a business, the desired outcome is a purchase from the client. For a parent, the desired outcome is for a child to do their chores without threatening a world war. Buyers say "yes" when perceived value exceeds the asking price. An effective "sales pitch" presents information in a compelling way so that happens with ease.

Selling starts with a persuasive appeal to the heart. Branding of logos, displaying of products, explaining of benefits, highlighting of outcomes, and building of value are all part of the persuasion process. When dollars make sense, the client says yes.

Selling continues with motivation. The motivation to buy includes identifying the need, explaining a solution, and asking for agreement. This final step of seeking a purchase should explain how the deal is a win-win for both the business and the buyer. This is the appeal to the mind.

A sales presentation could be a display at a local retail shop, a cold call offering a service, or a face-to-face meeting with a live demonstration of how something works. At its core, selling is nothing more than a transference of emotion. As feelings flow, agreement grows. Haven't you said "no" to someone who bored you to tears and said "yes" to a person who appealed to your soul? People often buy when emotions are swayed. And when someone has strong conviction, more deals will close. Conviction is key. This means that belief in the product must be strong. Think of the conviction that a politician has as she takes her message across the nation to run for a high office. She knows her slogan, has memorized stump speeches, believes she is the best answer for the country, and has passion for her vision. It's this type of conviction that sways voters and will sway people to buy pretty much anything. History is full of stories of people with conviction who were martyrs for their faith or who took a stand for social justice. The conviction you have as you talk about your company can add energy or cause the conversation to fall flat. Conviction is key.

Sales is the most important skill you will ever learn because it is the essence of communication. For greater business results, just fall in love with the craft of selling. Find books, podcasts, blogs, videos, and other resources to ensure you are selling every day. Learn from the old man and don't be a bum – sell something every day!

GIMMICKS WON'T WORK

We all know the day… "Black Friday." It comes yearly for our wallets and our attention. It is called this because it is traditionally the time that most retail outlets begin posting a profit. This is often the day that retail shop owners pull themselves out of the red of debt from the previous year. This is an odd moniker as the date is also synonymous with big discounts and enticing offers. How can selling something for less money produce a profit? Well, technically price reductions only work on a large scale. With volume, the pennies may add up. It takes a massive number of transactions to fill in the loss to the profit margin of highly discounted transactions. The companies that take a hit on a hot ticket item must also hope the loss is counteracted by add-ons and repeat clients. Yes, Black Friday is great for customers, but it is not so wonderful for the bottom line of a business. Maybe it should be called "Gimmick Friday" as it's on this day that advertising stunts are everywhere.

Modern consumers are smart enough to notice bait and switch promotions that lure them into the store and then change the offering. To the normal buyer, those "limited quantity" items are more of a frustration than a saving. Downloading a smart phone app for each business is annoying. And camping outside a shop to be the first to enter is so 2010. Yes, everyone loves a great deal, but gimmicks don't usually build raving fans.

Don't be fooled. Discounts are simply not an effective way to track the effectiveness of a marketing campaign either. For every single coupon redeemed, there are potentially thousands of impressions made which are never credited to the ad. Only a few people will ever mention they heard your commercial and even less will accurately remember where they noticed it. For any marketing, an "I saw your ad" response should really be considered an exception and not the norm. It just doesn't happen. Even if a coupon has tremendous response, it only reveals a handful of people who actually saw the coupon. We all know that receiving a coupon doesn't mean that you are going to redeem it, therefore we all know that coupons aren't a good example of how to track anything.

The idea of a QR code, special phone number, or coupon may seem like an effective solution for tracking advertising, but such thinking is flawed. Why test a marketing medium by giving away your own profit? How is it rational to judge an advertising campaign from the few sales directly generated by a public with an 8 second attention span? Doesn't it seem counterproductive to give something away so you can "track" an advertising's reach?

Think about it. Wouldn't most businesses rather attract a higher end customer? Affluent clients who spend more per transaction are definitely more attractive than a thrifty shopper who bounces from store to store looking for a better deal. Upscale clients don't want to mention seeing an ad, haggle, or clip a coupon. And from a buyer's perspective, who wants to shop at a store that is always running a daily sale or constantly going out of business?

There is a way to promote your business to clients who will pay good money for a great product or service. It's called branding. The more your brand is seen, the more you are recognized. The more you are recognized, the more people will trust you with their hard-earned money. Branding is not an exact science, yet we can learn from other businesses that it only works long term with repetition. Branding is like compound interest that grows over time. The aesthetic qualities of images, colors, fonts and even texture help establish your brand.

You can choose how your company is thought of. Would you rather be known as having great services with fair prices or be remembered for pesky gimmicks like Black Friday limited time offers?

JUST DON'T DO IT

There's only one way to build your business, and it has nothing to do with your product, service, or traditional advertising. You must make an emotional connection with consumers. And to do this, you must promote your business with frequency.

Yes, frequency is important because it builds relationships. If you only tell your partner, "I love you," a few times over a decade, the marriage will not go very well. And it doesn't work to run an ad quarterly. Marketing that creates emotional connections makes a purchase decision a no-brainer. This is where frequency enters the buying cycle. The more a brand is seen, the more a desire is created, the more trust is built, and the more your company grows in value. People see thousands of ads each day, so your frequency with an emotional connection will make the difference.

If the right people don't know who you are, then they can never choose you over your competition. "Saying I don't do any advertising" is a lie as every company advertises at least twice in its lifetime - once when it opens and once right before it closes for good. It's your decision when you market your company. To stay relevant and top-of-mind, you must keep your brand visible. And then repeat that message over and over again with feeling. One way to do this is to have a campaign that places your logo next to family-friendly content. That emotion created with feel-good stories transfers to your brand automatically. It takes time to grow positive emotion toward your brand so frequency can work.

In 1885 (yes, 1885) Thomas Smith published *Successful Advertising*, and in that work, he made the following reflection on effective frequency:

The 1st time people look at an ad, they don't see it.

The 2nd time, they didn't notice it.

The 3rd time, they are aware that it is there.

The 4th time, they have a fleeting sense that they've seen it before.

The 5th time, they finally read the ad.

The 6th time, they thumb their nose at it.

The 7th time, they get a little irritated with it.

The 8th time, they think, "Here's that confounded ad again."

The 9th time, they wonder if they're missing out on something.

The 10th time, they ask their friends or neighbors if they've tried it.

The 11th time, they wonder how the company is paying for all these ads.

The 12th time, they start to think that it must be a good product.

The 13th time, they start to feel the product has value.

The 14th time, they start to feel like they've wanted a product like this for a long time.

The 15th time, they start to yearn for it because they can't afford to buy it.

The 16th time, they accept the fact that they will buy it sometime in the future.

The 17th time, they make a commitment to buy the product.

The 18th time, they curse their poverty because they can't buy this terrific product.

The 19th time, they count their money very carefully.

The 20th time prospects see the ad, they might buy what it is offering.

THE BILL GATES PROPHECY

Life was different in 1996. *Independence Day* was the biggest movie of the year followed by the *The Nutty Professor*. The average cost of a new home was about $118,000 and gas was just above a buck a gallon. It was in that year that Bill Gates peered into his looking glass and made an amazing prediction that has come to pass. Gates said, "marketing is going to change, and content will be king." He said that the benefits of marketing would be generated from engaging content, instead of just display advertising. Fast-forward and today, we know that Gates was correct.

Content makes marketing valuable because of how it bonds your brand to the public. This can be accomplished through an advice video you post online or a blog article that gives out industry secrets only you know. It can also come through emotionally charged stories or photos that surround your ad. Yes, the media that encircles your logo affects emotions. A feel-good story makes people feel-good about you! The psychology of advertising aligns emotions with brands – your mind thinks certain things when you consider Nestle, Uber or Audi. Do you trust those companies? Do you like them? What do people think of your company?

Content drives brand awareness and builds trust in your business. It links your brand emotionally to the public. It lets you express your brand's personality and enhances the audience's view. In our modern world, the average person sees about 5,000 advertising expressions every single day. Of those logos, commercials, jingles, and ads, how do you differentiate your brand from the other 4,999? The answer is... content!

No one would listen to a radio station with 55 minutes of commercials and only 5 minutes of music. And gone are the days of magazines with 100% ads or coupon offers. Content draws people into the advertising medium. When someone hears an engaging story or reads a positive post, they are more likely to be open to the brand sponsoring the content. Subject matter marketing (not advertorials) drives awareness as it allows you to literally place your words into the minds of the reader.

There are cheap ways to advertise. It really isn't expensive to go from the mailbox to the trashcan. And it costs only pennies to run an ad on TV or radio at times when no one is tuned in. Cheaper is not always better! Successful marketing helps your business move from short-term to long-term memory. No form of marketing can create a need for your product or service. All advertising can do is give recognition so that when someone has a need, they think of you. Content marketing is the vehicle for that recognition. When Bill Gates used his crystal ball in 1996, he saw what we know today to be true – "content is king."

Here are a few ideas of content marketing...

- blog posts or articles submitted to local publications

- email newsletters

- social media posts

- podcasts

- video content

- webinars or in person workshops

- infographics

- mentorships or apprenticeships

- user-generated or interactive content

- behind the scenes tools or tips

SMALL WINS
FOR
BIG GOALS

It's been said that new year's resolutions are made to be broken. This observation is true, and it's kind of sad. Too many times, we resolve to do better with life and business, but then life and business get in the way. A few days into the new year, we are back to our old selves. It doesn't have to be like this! Big goals can be accomplished, and resolutions can be kept. How? With small wins. A small win is just that – a tiny accomplishment that might normally go unnoticed but, if it is celebrated, can build to a large victory.

Imagine that someone offers you ten million dollars if you can eat an entire African elephant. Would you take up that challenge with enthusiasm or be defeated and see it as totally impossible? The way to eat an elephant is the same way to reach your business goals – a little bit at a time (and a little bite at a time.) Determining what matters most is primary. Then have the end in mind so you can work backward.

What are your dreams, desires, and dares? What do you want to achieve? Why is that important? Who should be included in these pursuits? What needs to be done? How can you measure progress? When are the deadlines? The answers to these questions can help boil that elephant down to a realistic size. That huge and heavy animal of a goal can be chewed down daily.

Let's say you have a sales goal of $100,000 in one month. That seems huge until you chunk it down into bite-sized actions. You might not think you can do 100k in one month but that's only $25,000 a week, about $3,300 a day, $588 an hour, or about $10 a minute. Isn't that doable?

Know what targets are important to your business, divide the work into measurable actions, and then celebrate those baby steps.

A best practice is to keep a "wins journal" of the positive things that happen in your pursuit of greatness. This is a simple running list of obstacles overcome or steps taken along the way to success. Nothing is too small to be documented! Every "little" action counts! Return to this wins journal when you feel frustrated or just need to be reminded of how far you've come.

A study by renowned author and Ivy League Business School Professor Teresa Amabile found that small wins make bigger goals much easier to achieve because they help boost motivation and self-confidence. Progress and not perfection will lead to more resolutions being fulfilled.

Here's a guide to setting goals that can be accomplished.

- Decided what you really want. Ask yourself the "why?" question to determine the motivation behind such a target.

- Create a visual of achieving the target. Gather pictures of what achievement looks like and place them in your line of sight. Write out a celebratory mantra to repeat as you work.

- Break it down! Chunk your big objective into small bites. Make an outline of milestones that can be accomplished on the way. Know these targets and take pressure off yourself.

- Establish habits of achievement. Track your progress. Look at the movement along the way. Keep a "wins diary" or running list of accomplishments. Focus on the trajectory towards your goal instead of the total achievement.

- Celebrate regularly. Reward yourself and your staff as you pass the milestones. A small incentive makes a huge difference for future production.

Because you have decided to do better, you will get better. Don't pile on the pressure. Celebrate tiny wins. Resolve to eat that elephant, and your goals will become a reality.

ADVICE FROM THE EASTER BUNNY

In an exclusive interview, the one and only Easter Bunny gives advice for your business. What works to market your company? Let's see what the cottontail has to say:

"Thanks to word-of-mouth, everyone knows me, but that doesn't mean that my marketing should stop. If I don't keep myself in front of people, they might forget about me, of all people! This is why you see so many bunnies and candies around springtime. It's not enough to have name recognition. Even the world's most famous hare needs constant awareness. Local companies should leverage local advertising avenues to reach local residents. And never think you should ever stop marketing. Once you take a pause, you open the door for your competition to take your place. There's no way I'm going to allow some spring gnome to replace me," explained the Easter Bunny. Indeed, advertising helps businesses maintain brand awareness, even during periods of reduced sales or market downturns. By keeping their brand in front of their target audience, businesses can remain top-of-mind and stay relevant in their industry.

"Life is so busy, and people are distracted more than ever before. Commitment to an advertising campaign is how I can break through the noise of spring breakers and family vacations. Even pollen and wild weather try to steal my headlines. If I were to disappear from the shops, coloring pages, and baskets, then I would literally disappear. My big ears need to be seen so I'm not forgotten," the bunny continued, "being visible reminds people of the Easter holiday. Effective marketing programs mix multiple media types, like print and digital, with multiple

[120]

impressions. The more the public sees chocolate carrots, the more the public wants to eat chocolate carrots. Repetition works!" Advertising is important for new clients and for retaining existing clients. By communicating with prospects on a regular basis, businesses can keep them engaged and informed about new products or services, special offers, and promotions. By using the same branding and messaging across all platforms, you can ensure your customers have a consistent and positive experience with your brand, both online and offline.

"Consistency is key. I've never missed an Easter morning. Year after year, I hop all over to bring happiness to kids. A business shouldn't expect much in return if they only run quarterly ads or have sporadic advertising. Staying top-of-mind is how families know when you expect a visit from me. Don't hop around and try one marketing medium after another. Give a program time to build recognition. That's how I'm always recognized - I've never aged a day. I look the same as I did decades ago. Keeping a marketing message the same helps the message solidify into the public's memory," said the Bunny.

Indeed, it seems success in building your brand doesn't take a lucky rabbit's foot. Focusing on your target market and remaining visible builds recognition and an egg-traordinary future for your company. Advertising can help adapt to changes in the market, such as new competitors, shifting consumer preferences, or changes in technology. By regularly evaluating your advertising efforts and making adjustments as needed, your company can stay ahead of the curve and remain competitive.

Take this advice from the Easter Bunny for a basket full of business in your future.

THE HIDDEN INflUENCE OF EMOTIONAL ALCHEMY

The beer industry was in a drunken uproar in the Spring of 2023. Belgium destroyed a shipment of American Miller High Life after taking exception to its slogan of being "The Champagne of Beers." The country said the drink was improperly labeled as "champagne" and would not be sold as such. Drama also brewed around Budweiser as Bud found itself in the middle of a culture war. Two major corporations lost billions (billions!) of dollars because of marketing decisions. If this can happen to them, then it can surely happen to a local brand. How? Well, the public pairs businesses with the people and places where the brand is experienced.

If people find your ad on a news channel that's full of controversial opinions, they will just assume the talking heads speak for your company. Place your logo next to a feel-good story and that gooey feeling is transferred to your business. A coupon clipper can possibly cheapen your image while a big media buy can help your shop seem larger than life. An ambassador who talks up your brand could be good or bad - depending on how the public sees them. You don't need to be an alcoholic to learn this lesson of "sensation transference."

"Sensation transference" is a psychological phenomenon in which the emotions and feelings associated with one object or experience are transferred to another object or event. This phenomenon is widely used in marketing and advertising to create an emotional connection between the consumer and the product or service being marketed. Surely you can think of brands that elicit strong emotional ties and it's these emotional links that make marketing so powerful – for the good or the bad.

Marketers use various tactics to build this connection, such as emotional appeals, storytelling, and creating a brand personality. Sensation transference takes this connection to another level by creating an emotional association between the consumer and the product. Think of Chick-fil-A or Goodwill and those emotions that swell are the result of marketing sensation transference. Consider a commercial for a luxury car. The ad may show a car driving on an open road with beautiful scenery in the background. The viewer may feel a sense of freedom and exhilaration while watching the ad. These emotions become associated with the car in the viewer's mind, and the viewer may be more likely to buy the car because of this emotional connection.

Sensation transference can also work in reverse. If a consumer has a negative experience with a brand, they may transfer those negative feelings to the product. For example, if a person has a bad experience with customer service from a company, they may associate those negative feelings with the product and be less likely to buy it in the future. Aren't there places that you refuse to shop? That's sensation transference at work!

Another important factor in sensation transference is imagery. The colors, shapes, and symbols used in branding can create an emotional connection with the consumer. For example, Budweiser quickly rebranded from progressive social media posts to American nostalgia. A fiasco of marketing mistakes led the company to change their commercials to show the iconic Clydesdale horses galloping through all-American landscapes, with men grabbing a couple of cold ones together. And Miller High Life is having to rethink their choice in terms of libations. What you say, who you promote, and where your business is advertised does indeed matter. This is a lesson you can learn without a controversial beer bottle.

THE MOTIVATION MYTH

After the young couple were married and experienced the thrill of the honeymoon, the bride immediately called her mother. Her mom asked her how the honeymoon went, and the girl's answer was telling. She said in a panic, "The honeymoon was amazing. It was romantic and sweet. But as soon as we returned to our new home, my husband started using the ghastliest language, saying things I'd never heard before! He began to say these awful four-letter words! You've got to come get me and take me home from this toxic relationship. Please help me, Mom."

Shocked, her mother tried to calm the daughter by asking, "Tell me, what could be so awful? What four-letter words?" Still sobbing, the daughter whispered between tears, "Oh, Mom, he keeps saying things like dust, wash, cook, iron, and work." W-O-R-K. This four-letter word is too often considered a dirty curse. Who wants to get out of bed and punch a clock, anyway? Well, we were created to work. It's through our vocation that we can often find and express significance as our efforts offer opportunities to impact others. A meaningful job combines three key elements:

1) Significance – this is understanding how what you do benefits others.

2) Identity – this is knowing what the work makes possible.

3) Strengths – this is utilizing your strengths to get the job done.

Indeed, it is fulfilling to find a role that allows each of these areas to blend into daily activities. There is nothing like the feeling of fulfillment that comes from finding meaningful work. And while the emotion of making a difference is satisfying, man cannot live by emotion alone. Action – not inspiration – is what eventually gets the job done.

[124]

Business can be thrilling and frustrating. The highs are in the clouds, and the lows are below the deep. To make matters worse, disappointment sets in when inspiration flees. A dangerous motivation myth is an accepted lie that propagates that action comes after and only after feeling inspired. Feeling motivation is great, yet it cannot be your driving force. If it is, then an absence of motivation will drive you bonkers while your business suffers. Moments of inspiration should not be considered the standard; otherwise, you will rarely pursue excellence. Work, yes, that four-lettered word, must be the standard for success. And its doing the work that fuels true motivation.

"The only place success comes before work is in the dictionary," said Vince Lombardi. If you must wait to be motivated before you start, then you will probably never start. Motivation manifests most of the time only AFTER work has begun. Action often paves the way for inspiration to take more action. You must act your way to motivation. (Yes, fake it until you make it!) And the key to having consistent action is discipline. Most people don't really need motivation – they need to be disciplined to do the right things at the right time. The muscle of disciple pushes you to action even when you don't feel like it.

Best-selling author James Clear says that to "feel" motivated, then you should simply schedule it. "If your business doesn't have a system for marketing, then you'll show up at work crossing your fingers that you'll find a way to get the word out (in addition to everything else you have to do). Setting a schedule for yourself seems simple, but it puts your decision-making on autopilot by giving your goals a time and a place to live. It makes it more likely that you will follow through regardless of your motivation levels. And there are plenty of research studies on willpower and motivation to back up that statement," Clear continued, "Stop waiting for motivation or inspiration to strike you and set a schedule for your habits. This is the difference between professionals and amateurs. Professionals set a schedule and stick to it. Amateurs wait until they feel inspired or motivated." Don't let that foul four-letter word of W-O-R-K stop you. Action brings more action, and action brings motivation.

DOES HARVARD REALLY KNOW BEST?

The graduates of Harvard University become presidents, CEOs, and visionaries. Harvard also produces a regular publication that digs into business, culture, psychology, and other areas of professional life. Their "business review" is a trusted resource referenced and revered by readers. One startling discovery they documented is regarding how people make buying decisions.

After years of research, the *Harvard Business Review* uncovered and defined the buying process for every single purchase, from a candy bar to the new house. By understanding this flow, you can easily tap into the consumer's journey and place your marketing dollars at the most desirable point. This framework is called VACP and focuses on the key stages of the customer experience. VACP stands for: Viable, Acceptance, Consideration, and Purchase.

The first stage, **Viable**, refers to the need for businesses to ensure their products or services are relevant and desirable to potential customers. This requires businesses to conduct market research and customer feedback to identify and understand the needs and preferences of their target audience. For example, Sally selling seashells by the seashore is not really a viable business model – there are plenty of free shells that can be picked up at the ocean! You can't create a need, but you can capitalize on it. You must know your ideal prospect and current client.

The second stage, **Acceptance**, involves building brand awareness and credibility through marketing and advertising. This includes developing a strong brand identity, communicating the unique value proposition of the product or service,

[126]

and establishing trust with prospects. Here, you tell your brand story. For example, thanks to acceptance, most people immediately associate Colonel Sanders with Kentucky Fried Chicken.

The third stage, **Consideration**, focuses on providing potential customers with the information and resources they need to make informed purchasing decisions. This includes creating content and marketing materials that highlight the benefits and features of the product or service, and providing customer support and resources to help customers navigate the decision-making process. Investment in marketing has its greatest return of awareness at this point. For example, Spotify creates annual personalized content called "Wrapped." This is true content marketing – videos, graphics, and even playlists of someone's most listened to artists and songs. The "Wrapped" content can be enjoyed and shared on social media to elicit conversations. People see this and want to join Spotify or keep their membership.

The final stage, **Purchase**, involves optimizing the sales process to maximize conversions and drive revenue. This includes streamlining the purchasing process, offering flexible payment and delivery options, and providing excellent customer service and support. For example, the Domino's pizza mobile app easily allows you to order, add on products, save your favorite pies, collect loyalty points, and even track your delivery.

Overall, the VACP framework provides a comprehensive view on the entire customer journey, from initial awareness and consideration to final purchase and beyond. Which areas of VACP deserve your attention? How could your profit increase if you improved on just one of these 4 aspects?

The *Harvard Business Review* is right. The VACP flow of thought and action applies to every purchase regardless of the product. By knowing and using the framework of VACP, you can approach marketing in an effective way.

IS PRINT DEAD?

While watching an old movie, it's an odd sight to see people reading the newspaper or listening intently to the radio hour. Society and media have changed so much over the years. Can you imagine not having instant access to national news or the latest trends? Having the internet at your fingertips has ushered in the digital age to affect every part of life. When you want to know something, you can just ask Siri or Google. This is vastly different from the golden age of newsprint when advertising was easy – just run something in the daily reader for the entire town to see. The changes in life make you wonder if print is still an effective method of marketing. The answer isn't black and white.

A study conducted by *Forbes Magazine* proved that print materials and publications offer your prospects a brand experience that can't be replicated online. Because print is tangible, your brain subconsciously views it as credible. Print lasts to give your business lasting impact. The shelf-life of print is literally endless. Just consider how people keep boxes of photographs to revisit while their phone's photo roll is full of forgotten pictures. A recent poll of magazine readers found that an astounding 30% of readers never throw out their magazines. Compare this to how quickly someone scrolls past a post on social media, and you get the point. Isn't it nice to actually hold a book in your hands instead of just reading on a tablet? Print is actual "real estate" that can be picked up time and time again. Brochures, posters, and other physical items extend farther than most people think. We've all noticed weathered paper billboards that have survived for years.

Print is credible because it lasts. It takes caution and time to have all the facts, figures, names, and feelings just right in a story before it is published. Once the article goes to press, it's almost impossible to rectify any errors. Compare that to how quickly a tweet or blog post can be changed, and you'll see why people trust the written word. Even scribes of ancient manuscripts like the Bible had to be cautious of mistakes when hand copying. Penned publications have a permanent place in society.

Print is highly effective at leaving a lasting impression when a message is repeated over an extended period of time. This is different than other marketing media where you might hear a radio commercial several times throughout a week or see the same digital ad on many occasions in one day. Print takes time to build an effective return of recognition. 3 months of print advertising in a church bulletin might sound like a lot but that's only a few times the ad has been inserted into the bulletin. The longer the print is seen by the prospect, the more powerful it becomes. According to printisbig.com, advertisers in the United States spend on average $167 per person on direct mail to earn $2,095 worth of goods sold. That's a 1,300% return on investment.

While powerful, we can't ignore how traditional print has suffered as society has changed. Old print, with yesterday's news, may indeed be dead. Why pay for something you can get for free? The old is new again though with "hyper-local" publications. Hyper-local print is a blast from the past style newsletter or magazine that connects neighbors with homegrown information and interaction. It's a strong way to reach targeted clientele with feel-good stories by and for the neighbors. This type of "social media in print" is becoming more popular as time goes on. Community magazines leave a deeper emotional footprint in the brain. A study by Millward Brown found engaging with a physical piece of paper improves recognition and recall. Physical material – paper – is more "real" to the brain and engages its spatial memory networks. Even today, if done smartly, print is an effective tool to broadcast your business.

HOW TO MAXIMIZE PROfiT

Wouldn't it be great to have a business idea, hang a neon open sign, and see customers flow in with their credit cards in hand? We all know that this scenario is unrealistic. It takes blood, sweat, tears and marketing to succeed.

"An ad campaign focused entirely on getting leads is the least effective type of campaign you can run. Five things dictate a company's profit: the number of leads, closing percentage, customer usage, revenue-per-transaction, and profit margin. Of the five, the number of leads is the most difficult to track, the hardest to manipulate, and the one with the most negligible impact on profit. Ironically, a campaign focusing on any of the other four elements will automatically increase the number of leads," said business coach of the JP Revolution, John Preston.

Success requires hard work and an understanding of the 5 parts of profit.

Profit Part 1: New leads – novel clients who have never used your services. Everyone loves a new customer, and this is easily an area of profit. The more new customers you acquire the better off your bottom line can be. This area is often the focus of marketing yet is not the only reason to advertise. Too many companies fail because they only market and cater to new clients and forget about the other 4 areas of revenue. There's more profit available for you!

Profit Part 2: Repeat clients – much more cost effective than finding a new customer. Existing customers already like you! Just consider how your bottom line could explode if your existing customers used you more. You can tailor a marketing program to discuss additional services, sales, and benefits of shopping with you. A discount or incentive for repeat purchases brings more repeat purchases.

Advertise to keep your current clients or your competition may easily steal them from you!

Profit Part 3: Closing percentage – this is how often you turn a prospect into a buyer. Phone calls or clicks from advertising leads are great, but they need to translate into transactions. Coupons are not the answer. Coupons are the fool's gold of business. Give away your knowledge and expertise instead of giving away profit. Closing percentages increase when buyers trust your business. You will attract prospects by teaching through blog posts, social media videos, podcasts, and content marketing. Each interaction with the public can build trust so people say "yes" to your company.

Profit Part 4: High margins – cut expenses and increase sales to make this area lucrative. Knowing your profit and loss numbers allows you to identify opportunities. Higher margins can be affected negatively by inflation and affected positively by marketing. Focus promotions on those items that have the greatest earning value. Be smart with purchasing and positioning products. Market those greater margin areas and your checkbook will thank you. Run a smart business that highlights your strengths!

Profit Part 5: Total ticket sales – package products to add on additional revenue. Having complimentary choices benefits the buying experience. Offer items that make you the obvious choice for the complete package. Marketing is key for this area as you want to specifically pursue those who can use, need, and afford what you have to offer. Fast food chains understood this and added a drink and fries with their entrée for combo meals. How can you increase ticket totals with extra items? Market to those who can pay for more and you'll receive more!

There are five areas of profit for your business and increasing in each one by only 20% could lead to your company seeing a 100% rise in profit! Your business needs more than just new customers. You also need repeat clients, increased total ticket sales, high margins, and a healthy closing percentage. Generating new leads is only one-fifth of the possible profit! The five factors of profit are universal and when utilized can greatly impact your business. By understanding and utilizing the five parts of profit, you can ensure your business stays viable for many years to come. And you'll probably need less blood, sweat or tears!

FWB:
FEATURES WITH BENEfiTS

A new building was opening, and one of the owner's friends sent flowers for the occasion. The flowers arrived at the site and the owner read the card. It said, "Rest in Peace." The owner was angry and called the florist to complain.

After explaining the obvious mistake, the florist said, "Sir, I'm really sorry, but rather than getting angry you should imagine this: somewhere there is a funeral taking place today, and they have flowers with your intended note saying, "Congratulations on your new location." This was a bad mistake.

Another horrible mistake is when businesses fail to answer the "so what?" question that prospects are always asking. So what if your items are on sale? So what if you have award winning customer service, organic produce, or new technology? So. What.

Businesses blunder because they fail to communicate why prospects should care about their offerings. It's much more effective for the medical spa to say, "so you can look years younger" than boringly listing the features of Botox, b-12 injections, and dermal fillers. Advertising benefits, and not just features, are a proven way to win over prospects because it explains how your product makes life better.

A feature is what the product does. A benefit is what the feature does for the consumer. The features of purchasing a new refrigerator are endless BUT none of them matter if there's not a direct benefit. So what if the fridge can connect to Wi-Fi? So what if the design has more space? Well, the Wi-Fi can communicate when items are running low, and the spacious design can hold more food for less trips to the grocery.

"Here's what our product can do" and "Here's what you can do with our product," sound similar but are completely different approaches," said Jason Fried.

Too many advertisements are focused solely on features without connecting the dots to the bigger question of "why?" Companies are many times so proud of their features that they often forget what it will do for the customer! Consider the marketing of a mattress company. They could have an ad that shouts, "buy a mattress on sale." Or it could connect emotionally with benefits by saying "get your best night's sleep" or "you'll never want to get out of bed." The benefit is the end-result from the features. Features are for logical understanding while benefits appeal to emotions.

One key way to communicate benefits is to use a simple phrase - "so you can." This magical incantation turns a feature into a true selling point by meeting a need. "So you can" answers the "so what" question that your client is silently asking. For example, "the umbrella has a 5-foot span so you can stay dry in a downpour." Or "the car is hybrid so you can save money at the gas pump while you help the environment."

It's been said to "sell the sizzle and not the steak." This means the benefit of the sound, smell, and experience of the sizzle is more enticing than just the feature of eating a T-bone. The prospect will only buy when they understand how the benefit will improve their life. Don't make the mistake of placing features first or sending the wrong bouquet of flowers to the wrong location.

FOOLS FALL FOR FOOL'S GOLD

A cry of anguish was heard around the world when the news spread that Bed, Bath & Beyond was closing forever. How could this retail giant fail, people wondered? The answer is simple – they literally gave away their profits. Their business model, solely founded upon direct response marketing of coupons, dissolved like a bath bomb.

Coupons have long been a staple of marketing strategies for businesses looking to attract new customers and increase sales. However, the reality is that coupons are often the fool's gold of marketing, offering short-term gains at the expense of long-term profits. This type of marketing didn't work for Bed, Bath & Beyond and it won't work for you.

Coupons are often viewed as an easy and effective way to find prospects. However, the reality is coupons can actually harm you in the long run. One of the main problems with coupons is that they create a price-conscious customer base. When a business offers coupons, prospects begin to associate that business with discounts, and may not be willing to pay full price for products or services in the future. Using coupons can often lead to attracting the wrong type of client. Coupon clippers aren't loyal – they will float from shop to shop for the best discount. Don't pick up the fool's gold of thinking coupons are good for tracking the effectiveness of an advertising campaign – they only track how much money you are losing.

In today's online society, it's super easy for people to find coupons or promo codes for items they were going to purchase anyway. Don't be cannibalized by

[134]

coupons! Furthermore, coupons can create a negative perception of a business' brand. When a business regularly offers discounts, it can be seen as a sign of desperation or a lack of confidence in the value of their products or services. Do you want people to think you are hurting financially or about to file bankruptcy? This can lead to a decrease in brand value and customer loyalty. Coupons can be an extremely expensive promotion when factoring in creation, printing, and distributing the actual price reduction itself.

Another issue with coupons is they can adversely affect profit margins. With each sale, the gross income is reduced, meaning you may need to sell more items or services to make up for the lost profit. In some cases, the cost of offering a promo code may even exceed the revenue generated from the coupon, resulting in a net loss for the business. Do you really want to give away your hard-earned profit?

Instead of relying on coupons, businesses should focus on building relationships with customers and creating a positive perception of their brand. This can be achieved through various marketing strategies, such as creating a unique and memorable customer experience, offering value-added services, and sponsorship.

An effective alternative to coupons is to offer loyalty programs. Unlike attracting one-time customers looking for a deal, loyalty programs create a base of dedicated clients who are willing to pay full price. These programs reward customers for their repeat business, creating a sense of loyalty and goodwill. You could also offer free samples or trials. This allows prospects to try a product or service before committing to a purchase and can be a highly effective way to convert potential customers into loyal shoppers. Bed, Bath & Beyond learned the hard way coupons aren't a sustainable way to build a business. Don't fall for that fool's gold!

Recession Proof Your Business

Did you know that you can recession proof your business, so you are successful no matter how the economy swings?

The key difference between those companies that shutter and those that survive hard times is one thing – targeted marketing. A company should advertise more (not less) when business is slower than desired. No business has ever grown by cutting its marketing spending. This isn't an opinion; it is a proven fact. "In the 1920s, Post was the category leader in the ready-to-eat cereal category. During the Great Depression, Post cut back its advertising budget significantly and rival Kellogg's doubled its advertising spend, investing heavily in radio and introducing a new cereal called Rice Krispies, featuring "Snap," "Crackle" and "Pop." Kellogg's profits grew by 30% and the company became the category leader, a position it has maintained for decades," wrote Brad Adgate in *Forbes*.

During periods of economic slowdowns, businesses often face the challenge of reduced consumer spending and increased competition. While it may seem counterintuitive to invest in advertising during such times, history has shown that strategic marketing efforts can actually be highly beneficial.

When money is tight it creates a highly competitive landscape as businesses vie for a smaller consumer spending pie. By investing in advertising, you can increase brand visibility and create a lasting impression in the minds of consumers. This enhanced brand awareness helps businesses stand out from their competitors and gain market share. A prime example of this is McDonald's, which launched a successful advertising campaign during the 2008 financial crisis, focusing on its affordable menu options and value-driven messaging. This strategy allowed the fast-food giant to strengthen its market position and experience substantial growth during the recession. Your company can survive if you are keeping your foot on the gas pedal - no matter what mood the economy is in.

During economic slowdowns, advertising costs tend to decrease due to reduced demand. This presents an opportunity for businesses to gain a competitive advantage by securing valuable advertising space at more affordable rates. Procter & Gamble (P&G) is a testament to the benefits of this strategy. In the 1990-1991 recession, P&G increased its advertising budget by 19%, investing heavily in promoting its brands while competitors pulled back. As a result, P&G saw a significant increase in market share, reinforcing the importance of maintaining or increasing advertising expenditures during economic downturns.

Advertising can play a pivotal role in stimulating consumer demand. By highlighting the value and benefits of their products or services, businesses can instill confidence in consumers and encourage them to make purchases. During the Great Depression of the 1930s, automobile manufacturer Chevrolet increased its advertising budget and launched an innovative installment payment plan. This strategic move resulted in increased sales, solidifying Chevrolet's market position and establishing the brand as a symbol of reliability and affordability.

An increase in the share of voice can lead to an increase in the share of the market. A downturn, recession, or even lockdown is the perfect opportunity to set a company apart. In the 1990-91 recession, Pizza Hut and Taco Bell took advantage of McDonald's decision to drop its advertising and promotion budget. As a result, Pizza Hut increased sales by 61%, Taco Bell sales grew by 40% and McDonald's sales declined by 28%.

Don't cut your marketing budget when your building rent is increased, the stock market tumbles, or clients are slow to act. Instead of pulling back, perhaps double or triple your current spending. Seriously. Consider advertising as a key investment during economic downturns, turning challenges into opportunities and paving the way for growth and prosperity.

[137]

8 WAYS
TO EXCEL

Business is a non-stop barrage of stress and challenges. If it's not a problem with product then it's issues of employees, like Kevin, being late. Kevin struggled to get up early in the morning and as a result was always late for work. His boss got fed up with his constant lateness and so threatened to fire him if he didn't get his act together. Kevin went to see his doctor who gave him a pill and told him to take it just before going to bed.

He slept very well and actually beat the alarm clock by two hours. So, he fixed himself a nice breakfast and drove happily to work, in plenty of time for the start of the workday. When he got there, he said, "Boss, that pill the doctor gave me actually worked!" His boss said, "That's all very well, but where were you yesterday?"

Running a successful business requires a combination of strategy, hard work, and effective management skills like putting up with the Kevins in life. Here are some tips to help your company be more effective:

1) **Define Your Vision and Mission:** You need to have a clear vision and mission statement that outlines your goals and objectives. This will guide decision-making and help you stay focused on what's important.

2) **Develop a Strategic Plan:** This will help you identify your business's strengths, weaknesses, opportunities, and threat so you can develop a plan of action to achieve your goals. This plan should include your business strategy, marketing ideas, and financial projections.

3) **Build a Strong Team:** Your team is the backbone of your business, and it's essential to hire the right people for the job. Look for individuals who are passionate about your industry, have the necessary skills or experience, and share your values and vision.

4) **Focus on Customer Satisfaction:** Happy clients should be at the forefront of your mind. Make sure you're providing quality products or services, listening to feedback, and addressing any concerns or complaints promptly.

5) **Monitor Your Finances:** Keep a close eye on your finances and regularly review your cash flow, expenses, and revenue. This will help identify any areas where you can cut costs, increase profits, or improve your bottom line.

6) **Stay Ahead of the Competition:** Be up to date on industry trends and developments and keep an eye on your competitors. Look for ways to differentiate your business from the competition and identify any gaps in the market that you can fill.

7) **Embrace Technology:** Technology can help streamline your operations, improve efficiency, and reach a wider audience. Consider implementing tools and software to automate tasks, manage your finances, and improve your marketing efforts.

8) **Continuously Improve:** Running an effective business requires a commitment to continuous improvement. Regularly evaluate your operations, processes, and strategies, and make adjustments as needed to ensure you're always moving forward.

9) **And one extra:** Look at marketing as the most important aspect of your business. Sure, you provide a fantastic product or service. Yet without people knowing about your business then that offering is literally useless. Your marketing needs constant attention!

YOU DON'T HAVE TO FAIL

Did you know the average small business has only a 30% chance of making it for 10 years? According to data from the Bureau of Labor Statistics, approximately 20 percent of small businesses fail within the first year. By the end of the second year, 30 percent of businesses will have shut down. By the end of the fifth year, about half are gone and by the end of the decade, only 30 percent of businesses will remain. That's a 70 percent failure rate. How sad.

There's another number that correlates closely with these failure rates – it's the percentage of dollars spent on marketing. The more your company invests in promotions, the higher the likelihood that you'll stay in business for years to come. "The average small business spends 1.08% of its revenues on advertising, with variations from industry to industry. For instance, retailers spend more (about 4%) while restaurants spend 1.93%," reports *Small Business Trends*. Viewed in context, it is easy to see that marketing is one of the largest factors of viability for a business. If you don't want to be part of that 70% who go belly-up then perhaps you should consider another number from a trusted source. The Small Business Administration (SBA) recommends starting with a marketing and advertising budget of at least 10% of gross revenue.

The SBA is a government agency that provides support and resources to small businesses across the United States. As part of its mission, the SBA offers guidance and advice to small business owners on a range of topics. They assist with business loans, education, and support. Their website is full of resources to be considered including many tips on how not to be one of the 7 of 10 companies that crack.

The SBA clearly believes that one of the most important steps in success is having an advertising and marketing plan. This involves identifying your target audience, setting marketing goals, and developing a strategy to reach your audience to achieve those goals. For year-over-year growth, the SBA suggests placing up to 20% of gross revenue into spreading your name throughout the community.

The association advises small businesses to focus on their unique selling proposition when developing their advertising and marketing strategies. This is the factor or feature that sets your business apart from competitors and makes it attractive to your target audience.

It's also recommended to use multiple channels to reach your target audience, including social media, email marketing, online advertising, print media, and events or trade shows. By using a variety of channels, you can reach an ideal audience and increase your chances of triumph.

According to the SBA, strong branding is essential to differentiate yourself from competitors and establish credibility with their target audience. It is key to develop a strong brand identity, create a consistent visual image tone of voice in all marketing materials. They also teach sponsorship of local events, cross marketing with other organizations, and following up with existing clients for referrals.

"A referral program could be as simple as giving a satisfied customer a few extra business card and asking them to refer their friends. Or you could offer a bounty (discount or award) to the referrer and even to the customer being referred. Say you're an interior designer. You could offer a $200 credit to past clients who refer their friends and an equal discount to the referred client," wrote Anita Campbell for the SBA.

In addition to these tips, the SBA also provides a range of resources and support those looking to improve their advertising and marketing efforts. These include online courses, webinars, and workshops, as well as access to financing and business counseling services. You can even work directly with an SBA counselor for no charge. Check out their website at sba.gov for more information on their program and how to ensure your company is one of 3 out of 10 that survive. You don't have to fail!

THE EFFECTS OF BUTTERfly AFFECT MARKETING

When a butterfly flaps its wings in Australia, that tiny change of air pressure could eventually cause a hurricane in the Atlantic Ocean - or at least this is the idea of the scientific chaos theory that shows how small trivial events could result in something ultimately much larger. "Butterfly Marketing" works exactly the same way by depending upon non-direct impressions to eventually lead to business growth. This concept takes the focus off the sale or the service and places it upon the people who are being sold to and serviced. Butterfly Marketing is all about transformational touches instead of transactional ones.

You can create a sense of belonging, build trust, and provide value as you engage to give back. When the community feels connected, they will begin to have a favorable opinion of your shop even before the sales process has begun. And like the wings of a beautiful monarch, there are two proven strategies that can have a lasting impact.

1) **Provide Value**

2) **Participate Regularly**

This may seem counterintuitive, but providing value is an opportunity to give away your expertise. A tutorial video or "how to" article gives useful content and relevant insights. An open house or even a food drive builds trust and loyalty toward your brand. Wouldn't you want to support a veterinary clinic that treats stray cats for no charge? Or how would you feel about a restaurant that provides meals for first responders each month? Butterfly marketing movements like these are genius.

Consider what questions customers commonly have about your store and answer them before they are asked. Share details of how you are involved in the town and how supporting you supports a greater good. Get involved with non-profits, forums, or events to be seen as a viable part of the public.

Participating regularly fosters relationships and can create brand advocates who will promote your business to others. Visibility leads to credibility. And credibility brings profitability. Consistent messaging of "we're here and we care" can have huge bearing upon tomorrow's cash register. Like a caterpillar transforms into a butterfly, your business can be transformed when you give back your knowledge!

Knowing whose interests are being served is the key element to identifying if you are flying with the butterflies. Take for example how your company could go beyond driving traffic to your social media pages and begin to drive social change locally. You are telling a story as you engage in conversations, offer opinions, give testimonials, highlight team members, share posts from important organizations, educate, and forward updates on projects. Pictures of interactions between clients and staff are memorable. Action on your social media gets on average 160% more attention when you use relatable images. Are you speaking the language of your community or do prospects only know you for your discounts or offerings? Providing value also includes regular communication. Staying top of mind can be accomplished with branding in local print, thank you cards, texts, email blasts, and asking for referrals. If focused on the client's concerns, social media can have tremendous impact.

Sadly, traditional marketing picks the sledgehammer instead of the gentle moth. By failing to tap into the emotional experience of the buyer, billions of ad dollars are wasted. Butterfly Effect marketing understands that today's consumer needs continual exposure in soft ways. It's a campaign – a long-term commitment to making a difference while you make a dollar.

A FEW DOS AND DON'TS OF ADVERTISING

Do...

- Define your brand's unique value proposition.

- Describe your perfect client and market only to them.

- Develop a strong visual identity, including a logo and regular color scheme.

- Create a consistent brand voice and tone for all marketing materials.

- Establish a clear message and mission statement.

- Monitor and respond to customer feedback to improve your brand.

- Understand that advertising can't guarantee results – it only builds recognition.

- Mix media with marketing on print, digital, audio, sponsorship, referrals, etc.

- Make giving your business 5-stars easy for happy clients.

- Expect a true campaign to take time to be effective.

- Have a budget of what to spend yearly, monthly, and weekly on marketing.

- Develop a plan to market to existing clients so your check average increases.

- Ensure your information online is correct across various platforms and websites.

- Involve your staff for ad design or photos.

- Get involved with the Chamber of Commerce, networking groups, and non-profits.

Don't...

- Be afraid to commit to long-term branding programs.

- Copy your competitors' marketing strategies.

- Assume instant overnight results.

- Neglect your online presence, including social media and website listings.

- Overcomplicate your branding message or visual identity.

- Think all marketing mediums work the same.

- Forget to ask for feedback and online referrals.

- Use offensive or insensitive language or imagery.

- Advertise only for new clients or visitors to your store.

- Ignore the importance of brand consistency across all channels and platforms.

- Expect marketing to be a magic wand that works instantly.

- Think of advertising as an expense that can be easily cut.

- Pass up good marketing ideas because your budget is spent.

- Fill your ads with wordy information and details.

USE THIS SECRET WEAPON

During World War II, a secret project called "Operation PLUTO" remarkably altered the course of history. A group of British scientists laid undersea pipelines across the English Channel to connect England and the Allied Forces in France. These hidden pipelines, placed under enemy-controlled waters, transported fuel supplies that were crucial for the Normandy landings and subsequent operations. This secret weapon was an engineering marvel. For your business, there's a similar secret weapon that works powerfully to create credibility and engage your audience – local magazines.

"The numbers show us that print magazines still get the attention of a niche audience. This means there's still return on investment (ROI) in magazine advertising. Magazines deliver higher return on investment on advertising spending across all media, averaging a $3.94 return on every dollar spent. That's 50% higher than all other categories. Nielsen looked at this as well and found magazines had the highest aggregate ROI over TV, online, online video, and outdoor. That's not just in the U.S., either; a European study found the same high rate of return for magazine advertising," wrote an article on www.sheridan.com. It may be difficult to quantify brand-building activities like magazine sponsorship, yet an increase in recognition and positive associations will eventually lead to higher engagement, which impacts the bottom line.

While ROI is impressive for print, what is more compelling is CLV. This acronym stands for Customer Lifetime Value. The CLV is highly elevated with local print. This means that clients tend to make repeat purchases and the overall importance of the client is raised. Yes, everyone wants a new customer, but repeat buyers are how you can stay in business long term.

One idea is to utilize local publications. These are often micro-targeted based on location, income level, or home ownership. The ads placed are hand-delivered in the mail to ensure the right people see the ad. As an essential link between the community and commerce, local magazines provide worthwhile content that can't be found anywhere else. The content is useful and trusted so prospects become comfortable with your company. Readers are also familiar with the other advertisers in the publication. Your reputation is immediately elevated when you are in a quality magazine with other reputable companies. A National Retail Federation study showed that shoppers are most likely to start an online search after viewing a magazine advertisement.

A neighborly newsletter is often interactive as well. Readers can often be found as the writers of the publication when the pages are filled with content from the community. Just imagine, if you were to submit a family recipe to be featured in a full-size, full-color magazine, wouldn't you read it and tell others about your feature? This is another area of value as local magazines are often written by the people and for the people.

The lasting effects of local magazines are convincing and impressive. Just consider how when readers pick them up, their full attention is on the page. There's no need to press buttons or be distracted. And someone can't hold a magazine and a cell phone at the same time – they have to focus on the text and advertisements. People reread local magazines and can see the advertisement over and over again, which is vastly different than online splashes that appear for just a few seconds. The secret weapon of a local magazine won't save a war, but it could save your company from wasting advertising dollars on gimmicks or direct-response options. With a high CLV, an impressive ROI, and targeted delivery through local magazines, your business can win any war.

The Tortoise Approach Wins

Children know the story of how the tortoise and hare were in a race for fame and fortune. The tale shows how the rabbit ran at lightning speed and jumped through obstacles. He got so far ahead that he stopped for a meal and a long luxurious nap. The turtle, slow and steady, pressed on and eventually passed his snoozing competitor. Consistency won the race in that fable, and it will be in your marketing as well. To have long-term business success, you need a long-term view of marketing. Keeping a consistent message over time will build your brand so you attract new clients and keep your existing customer base.

Consistent marketing should also include a mix of media. Sharing a repeated message across print and digital formats is one of the keys to successful advertising. Take a look at your ads in print and compare them to your digital ads. And consider what you say on the radio, in school sponsorships, at your location, or even your logos. Are the messaging and visual elements consistent between each of them? These elements of advertisements work well together to boost consumer retention. If you want potential customers to remember your business over the rest, focus on building a consistent ad campaign that taps into both print and digital media.

Some managers try to take the easy road to perceived profits by pulling advertising. They say they "can't afford to advertise" which is the same as saying they "can't afford to be in business." Marketing is not all or nothing. It should be all or something. Your company runs the risk of closure if you stop advertising. This isn't an idea – it is a proven fact. Research of over 70 Australian brands conducted over two decades found that when advertising was cut or even stopped that business blundered. "Brands saw their sales fall 16% after one year without advertising compared to the last advertised year, and by 25% after two years. By three years the drop reaches 36%, though as the years continue the steady decline eventually tapers off. Stopping advertising means brands cannot build or refresh mental networks through mass communication. Plus, other nudges come from buying or using the brand, seeing other people buy or use the brand, or seeing in-store displays and activations (which typically favor bigger brands)," the report by the Ehrenberg-Bass Institute says.

Do you want stable decline or stable growth? You don't need to be like the rabbit and exude all of your cash/energy at once in hopes to have speed. Consistency is key. "While it may be tempting to withdraw the advertising budget for a boost in profits, the evidence suggests that doing so risks putting the brand on a downward sales trajectory," wrote Michaela Jefferson in the report.

Sure, there are gimmicks or even the preposterous idea of stopping marketing that promise quick results. Direct response methods are like the racing rabbit and can seem to work short term. Your success isn't a temporary desire, though. Continued exposure provides continued results. The pace of the turtle proves that consistency wins.

YOU SIMPLY WON'T BELIEVE THIS

Does it ever feel like there's a hypnotic spell that's been placed on you which leads to certain purchases? Well, good marketing is not voodoo, but it does appeal to your inward parts? An Ivy League professor, Gerald Zaltman, says that 95 percent of our purchase decision making takes place in the subconscious mind. This means that what people buy has less to do with thinking and more to do with feeling. When an advertising program is geared towards the subconscious mind amazing things can happen.

"Based on advertising campaign performance, 31% of ads with emotional pull succeeded versus the 16% success of ads that focused on rational content. Themes of pride, love, achievement, friendship, loneliness, and memories perform best. An emotional response to an advertisement, rather than the ad's actual content, produces great influence on the intent of a consumer to buy a product. Likeability is the most predictive measure that can help ascertain if an advertisement will increase the sales of a brand," says the University of Southern California's Master of Science in Applied Psychology Program. For example, when the Apple Watch Series 7 was first advertised it evoked feelings of fear and relief. The commercial played recorded 911 distress calls which demonstrated the power of the Apple Watch to provide comfort and support during a crisis.

The most effective feeling in marketing has proven to be empathy. When someone has an empathetic response, they feel close to a brand. This is often accomplished through showing images of babies or pets in ads. Good feelings play a part as well. People buy when thoughts of better days or even dreams of the

[150]

future are given a platform. Netflix achieved this wonderfully with their billboards that said, "Don't give up on your dreams. We started with DVDs." This evoked feelings of perseverance and nostalgia.

Creativity is another game-change for brands. A creative marketing program builds an emotional rollercoaster that keeps consumers glued to the message. Just think of the creative ads from certain high-end car companies that work to keep you guessing what is next and you'll see how easily the subconscious mind can be tapped.

Jorge Barraza, Ph.D., Program Director and Assistant Professor in the online Master of Science in Applied Psychology program at USC notes that emotion is a core aspect of advertising. Advertisers can foster engagement by evoking emotions like nostalgia, which "can remind us of what it feels like to be loved and accepted, providing feelings of stability and comfort." Subaru accomplished this during a commercial that featured Frida, a paralyzed and abandoned dog that was rescued and put into braces, allowing it to walk again. Feelings of love and sympathy were evoked and the message of safety from Subaru was clearly communicated.

Emotions in advertising make businesses memorable, foster entertainment, create engagement, relate with authenticity, and increase a personable view of the business. This can be done with negative feelings, too. Some groups prefer "sadvertising" to evoke pity at the heartstrings of the consumer. Other emotions can be pulled with shocking facts, questions which are thought-provoking, concerning images, and meaningful content. "Marketers who incorporate certain emotional characteristics can increase emotions among consumers," says *Forbes*. Put some thought into your marketing and you may be able to sway the subconscious thoughts of prospects. No magic spell or witches broo needed!

BARBIE SHOWS US
HOW TO BE A SUCCESS

Even if you haven't seen the Barbie movie, it's practically guaranteed that you've heard of the flick. How can such a statement be made? Well, the studio behind the blockbuster actually spent more money on marketing the movie than filming it.

According to *Variety*, over $150 million has been invested in publicizing Barbie in every way possible, from television to radio, print and online. "The marketing campaign ranged from a website allowing fans to make custom "Barbie" posters, to partnering with insurance company Progressive for a commercial shot on the movie set, to teaming with Airbnb to create a life-size replica of Barbie's Malibu dreamhouse, and even collaborating with Burger King Brazil on a pink burger," said insider.com. Success was not left up to word of mouth, referrals, or one type of media.

This huge marketing campaign was a risk by Hollywood. It paid off with major results. Can you imagine spending more on marketing dollars than you put towards any other expense? What could happen to your business if you added up your entire cost of business for one month, and then budgeted more than that towards marketing the next month? The children's toy movie cost $145 million to film compared to the $150 million used to advertise it!

The Barbie producers believed in their product so much they risked their entire fortunes telling the world why the movie should be seen. And it worked. This gutsy move could work for local businesses, yet most managers are more concerned with risk than they are open to the possibility of reward. Too many penny-pinching

[152]

bean counters inhibit company growth by worrying about what might happen if the marketing doesn't work. The other idea - what could happen to business if an insane amount is invested in publicity - is rarely considered.

The team behind the Barbie movie calculated the risks and weighed the rewards. Their conviction in the film led to an amazing response from the world as Barbie had the biggest opening weekend of 2023 at the US box office. It also grossed more money than any other movie that year. Do you believe in your own business enough to do something similar?

It's easy to view marketing as an expense that can easily be cut because there is no true way to track its effectiveness. The same could be said for the rent, electric bill, or taxes. Can you track the return on investment of what you pay in employment taxes? Of course not! Advertising is the same way – it's a part of doing business that cannot be ignored, unless you want to fail. Consider your realistic expectations before starting any campaign and perhaps judge its effectiveness 9 to 12 months after it has begun.

It's time to stop playing with marketing like it were a kid's toy and learn from the Barbie buzz to really invest in your company.

YOU NEED THIS PYRAMID SCHEME

Pyramid schemes are notorious for growing a business idea so that money flows to the top earners without being fair to those on the bottom. What if there was a pyramid model that benefited everyone involved? Well, efficient branding works through a pyramid model. This idea resembles Pharoah's buildings more than the latest get-rich-quick trick. Here's how:

Shoppers want to choose an item or business they know. Awareness and trust are key to sway buying decisions. Consider the pyramid shape with a wide base that ascends to a pinnacle to understand how to best promote your company. At the base of the pyramid and at the start of a company's foundation is zero awareness. This is when your name is hardly known and potentially when your products are not desired. There's plenty of room to grow a strong base here, so don't let a lack of recognition stop your passion.

The next level of marketing is basic brand recognition. At this point, prospects begin to recognize your logo, packaging, services, colors, or slogan. Through consistent messaging you are able to start appealing to prospects. To get to this step takes delivery of an outstanding product or service as well as smart marketing.

The pyramid continues to ascend with instant brand recall. Here, all it takes is simple exposure or a mention of your name to elicit feelings. People will recall your company thanks to marketing, association, and conversation. Recall is necessary, as most advertising is experienced before the buying decision is made. People don't usually need your services or product the exact moment your commercial is seen. Most marketing is experienced by prospects before they have a desire or need. Brand recall occurs when your business jumps to an individual's mind when they require the products or services that you provide. It can also occur because of a conversation or association. For example, Gmail and Yahoo pops to mind when someone thinks of email. Sure, there is competition with other apps, but these two command attention.

The pinnacle of the pyramid is top-of-mind-awareness. This is when your service is first on the list of choices in someone's thinking. What companies come to mind when you think of computers, tennis shoes, sports cars, movie theatres, or baby food? Whomever you thought of is at the top of your pyramid. Consider Zoom for example. There are numerous video conferencing applications, yet it has been Zoom that has become a brand. Even if someone uses a different app, like a Meet or Team, they say "let's do a zoom." Top-of-mind-pyramid services are used frequently as buyers are loyal to their favorite brand.

How do you build your pyramid like the mighty Pharoah did? Well, you should start by telling your story. A story brand is your journey. It is how you impact lives. A story brand is greater than an offer or discount. It is a description of who you are and what you do. Sure, flashes of sales prices are nice but cheap deals don't build brands. Your narrative gives authenticity and explains the higher why of your ways. How would you describe your business? Do you state facts and figures or are you giving an emotional appeal to evoke feelings? A story brand is personal so consumers can connect with you and not just a faceless company. Know your story and keep it before you – post it at your office, in social media, and on your website. It's been said that a picture is worth a thousand words and that a story is a thousand pictures. Your brand narrative will allow your business to construct a pyramid of awareness. It doesn't take a scheme to be successful, it takes a story. It takes your story!

TWO WORDS TO CHANGE YOUR WORLD

What two words can impact your business in a powerful and effective way? You might say "on sale" or "sign here" or "you're hired." Those are good phrases, yet there is a simple comment that can surely create a better environment for your customers and employees. The two words are "thank you." This simple statement shouldn't be overlooked. It is fundamental to an abundant life and a thriving business as it expresses appreciation; that you value others. Feeling and expressing gratitude tells your clients that they are more than just a number. It says to your employees that they are more than just a paycheck.

Gratitude gives perspective and helps reframe challenging times. You can be grateful even when that sale doesn't go through, a customer is aggravating, an employee doesn't show, or stress mounts. So many times, we focus on the problems of the day and what we don't want. Nothing gets better by thinking about how bad it is. Instead, gratitude reminds you to be thankful for your business and its challenges (at least you have reason to pay those pesky taxes!). Frustration is inevitable but defeat is optional thanks to gratitude. How?

Scientists have proven that appreciation releases positive energy that can affect your work environment and even your body. Blood pressure is lowered, sleep is improved, smiles are shared, and even dopamine and endorphins are released when you say, "thank you." Gratitude lightens the mood and helps people be in a better attitude. Who wouldn't want that at work?

We all know what it's like to feel taken advantage of or unappreciated. However, as you feel and express gratitude it starts a domino effect that touches lives and even helps your company's bottom line. Saying "thank you" can cause profits to increase as employees give their best when they feel valued, and customers return when they are cherished. When you use these two words you are acknowledging the impact of others and creating a culture of abundance. Here are a few ways to express gratitude at work:

- Leave a personalized post-it sticky note where an employee can easily find it.

- Take time to listen and respond to clients. Ask questions to get to know them better. Find out what matters to them.

- Notice when a client or employee has an accomplishment and celebrate with them with a social media post or little gift.

- Have a pizza party for your staff or order their favorite dessert to be delivered while they are working a shift.

- Hold an event for the community. This can be a fun and informative way to give back and network at the same time.

- Handwrite and then mail a card to a few of your loyal customers thanking them for your support.

- Remember your employee's birthday or anniversary and make it special.

- Upgrade a purchase of a random client or bend the rules for that upset client to accommodate their requests.

A STEP-BY-STEP MARKETING PLAN

If you are stressed by just simply thinking about marketing, then you are not alone. Developing a marketing plan is a daunting task for most business leaders. With this step by step guide the anxiety is removed and your success is projected. Use this guide to help define your brand, determine your target market, decide on a platform, and deliver your message.

Consider the comments and answer these questions. You can create an effective and powerful plan to grow your company! It has been said that if you fail to plan then you plan to fail. Do not let your business suffer because you don't market your company properly.

Branding is remembering. To help establish and grow your brand you should market consistently and with repetition. This doesn't happen by accident. You need a plan and this plan to help people use your services or buy your products does not have to be complicated. It can be simple. The more touches your brand or logo has upon your target market, the more those customers are apt to think of you when they need you. The steps are...

- Define your brand

- Determine your target market

- Decide on a platform

- Deliver your message

[158]

To remove that stress, simply take time to think about your brand, target market, and platforms for delivery. And then put those thoughts into an action plan for growth.

Define Your Brand

- What is your company mission statement?

- What benefits do you bring to clients?

- How do you want to be remembered? What impression would you like to leave with the public?

- What value does your business contribute to the community and the world?

- What problems do you solve?

- What is your higher why or purpose for being in business? Why did you decide to do this business?

- How exactly does your service or product help others? Describe the process and the end result of how it works.

- What exactly do you provide? What are the details?

- What slogan or motto does your company have?

- If you could only share one message with your current and potential clients, what would you want to say?

- What is your "elevator pitch" quick explanation of your business that you give to others?

- Which colors define your message?

- What type of logo would deliver your brand effectively?

- What "story" does your brand tell?

- How can you make the client the "hero" of your brand story?

- Which causes or non-profits matter the most to your company?

- Businesses use color strategically to express identity, target specific types of customers and influence purchasing behavior. They can also use it to establish brand recognition and identity. Establishing a strong, recognizable brand can help influence consumer perception, purchase intent and buyer behavior. Certain colors are associated with feelings or characteristics. Pick colors that reflect your vision. For example...

  - Red is about passion, aggression, or power.

  - Blue shows serenity and calmness

  - White conveys purity.

  - Yellow is about energy.

  - Green reflects health and the environment.

Determine Your Target Market

- Describe your perfect customer in detail. What is their lifestyle? Where do they shop? What are their hobbies? What type of education or income do they have? What is their age range? Where do they live? What type of jobs do they perform?

- Describe your current clients? What is unique or meaningful about them?

- Who needs your services?

- Who can afford your products?

- Is this a global or local market?

- What organizations are they involved with professionally and personally?

- What mile radius from your center of business would you take customers?

- Who are the influencers in your target audience that could be utilized to support your business growth?

Decide on a Platform

- With your target market in mind, where do these people interact socially?

- Based on trends, research, and your perfect client's age, which type of media do they prefer?

- Does your target audience travel?

- Have you set up Google my business profile

- Is a website imperative for your clients?

- Which types of social media does your target audience use predominately?

- How can you use sponsorship to gently expose your company to the community?

- How can you utilize influencers to share your brand?

- How many different types of advertising can you utilize?

    - Broadcast radio or television

    - Direct mail

    - Billboards, ads on public transportation and other outdoor ads

    - Print, such as newspaper, brochures, flyers, and magazines

    - Product placement in films or TV shows

    - Word-of-mouth referral programs

    - Sponsorship of events or special causes

    - Digital display, such as pop-ups and banner ads

- o Digital mobile

- o Digital native search

- o Digital paid search

- o Digital podcasts

- o Digital social media

- o Digital videos

Deliver Your Message

- The goal of marketing is to become a household name, so your company is known, liked, thought of and used regularly. This is accomplished through connecting with your market emotionally with education, exposure, and energy.

- Marketing should be strategic with an understanding that business is a marathon and not just a sprint. A successful company takes time and successful branding takes time.

- If you want your company to be busy, then the best time to advertise is 6 months ago. The second-best time to advertise is now!

- Start small and don't get discouraged when results aren't instant. There isn't a guarantee when it comes to advertising except for recognition.

- Advertising cannot create the need for a product or service. Instead, it builds recognition so that when people need you, they think of your company.

- Buying decisions are often made based on top-of-mind-awareness. This is accomplished through continual exposure.

- How can you mix direct response with branding to grow awareness of your company?

- Content is king! Give back to your target audience with education and informed buyers will come your way.

- Automate your impressions as much as possible.

- Use a variety of mixed messaging.

- Commit to long-term consistent messaging and trust the process.

- Describe the values and benefits in your advertising. Cut out the "noise" of details. Less said is best said.

- Ask for referrals and start with your "hot market." Pick the "low hanging fruit" to build business awareness.

- Local networking groups provide opportunities to interact with decision makers and influencers.

- Online networking also works to contribute to conversations and be included.

- Pick one social media platform your target market uses and stick with it and then expand to others.

- Pick one networking group your target market uses and stick with it and then join others.

- How can you partner with a charity or non-profit for cause marketing?

- What are your projected gross sales for the year? From this number the Small Business Association suggests investing up to 20% of this number in marketing if you want to see growth in the next year. What is your yearly and monthly budget for advertising?

- What events can you hold or participate in to gather awareness of your brand?

ABOUT THE AUTHOR

Daniel Rendelman connects with people through inspirational writing, business coaching, speaking engagements, online content, and community leadership. Daniel is a certified John Maxwell Team speaker, coach, and leadership trainer. His experience as an entrepreneur has included time as a successful restaurant franchisee and operator of a large wireless company. Currently, Daniel is the publisher of three community magazines and is a division leader with Best Version Media, responsible for a team of publishers throughout the state of Georgia.

Daniel is an ordained minister and the author of 10 books, including three children's books. His 2019 work, "An Appreciation Awakening," was a featured finalist in the American BookFest awards.

He serves on several boards of directors in his local town in South Carolina including the Chamber of Commerce, Rotary, and a community grant foundation. He enjoys volunteering, learning to play the guitar, teaching, and a nightly bowl of ice cream.

Daniel is happily married to Sara, who is also his business partner. He loves being a father of nine children who fill his life with joy. Daniel's desire is to add value to the world by encouraging others to live their best life.

To learn more from Daniel visit www.marketingmattersbook.com.